It Takes a Village

Founded by CEO Michelle Kennedy, Peanut is one of the fastest-growing social-networking apps for women, listed as Apple's Trend of the Year 2021, TIME100's Most Influential Companies 2022 and Fast Company's Most Innovative Companies 2023. *It Takes a Village* is Peanut's first book, written and created alongside thousands of Peanut users from around the world.

It Takes a Village

And Other Essential Truths for New Mothers

PEANUT

with a foreword by Lorraine Kelly
and her daughter Rosie Smith

PENGUIN LIFE

AN IMPRINT OF

PENGUIN BOOKS

PENGUIN LIFE

UK | USA | Canada | Ireland | Australia
India | New Zealand | South Africa

Penguin Life is part of the Penguin Random House group of companies
whose addresses can be found at global.penguinrandomhouse.com.

Penguin Random House UK,
One Embassy Gardens, 8 Viaduct Gardens, London sw11 7bw

penguin.co.uk

First published 2025
001

Set in 13.4/16pt Garamond MT Pro
Six Red Marbles UK, Thetford, Norfolk
Printed and bound in India by Manipal Technologies Limited

The authorized representative in the EEA is Penguin Random House Ireland,
Morrison Chambers, 32 Nassau Street, Dublin D02 yh68

A CIP catalogue record for this book is available from the British Library

ISBN: 978-0-241-70998-6

For all mothers, everywhere

Contents

CONTENTS

Foreword

Hello from Lorraine

Throughout my career I've had the privilege of meeting thousands of women, each with their own remarkable story around motherhood, not to mention my own experience of being a mother to Rosie. In the thirty years since she was born things have changed so much, but despite the minefield of modern motherhood to be navigated she has become a brilliant mum. I have learned so much from her when it comes to my granddaughter Billie, and babysitting is now my favourite job in the world!

I remember feeling overwhelmed and lonely when Rosie was a newborn – none of my friends had children at the time and my own mum was so far away in Scotland. I think I just 'muddled through' those early months – with the help of Rosie's dad – but I still remember those feelings of loneliness and anxiety. Back then I had so many worries and questions: what the best room temperature was for a newborn, how long should her naps be, or how much should I feed her. I would leave her out in the garden in her pram to get some fresh air and then stress that she was going to catch a cold and bring her back inside again. I spent ages rocking her to sleep, only to wake her up to check she was still breathing. And I thought I must be the only mum who was doing that.

I convinced myself that people would think I was a bit daft for not knowing all the answers – how I would have loved the Peanut App myself back then! It's like having a whole group of supportive friends in the palm of your hand and I've seen the difference it's made to Rosie's journey into motherhood. But, most importantly, sharing the stories of these wonderful mums, and learning from each other, has the potential to bring so much comfort to so many. That's why this book is so special. Because it really does take a village to raise not just a child, but a mum and a granny too!

Love, Lorraine

Hello from Rosie

If you're reading this, I think I've been where you are now. I think I've stood in your shoes, and if I haven't yet, I'm probably about to. If you've just found you are pregnant and are standing in the parenting section of your local bookstore, I've been there. (And congratulations!) Or if your mum/best friend/partner has bought you this book because you have a new arrival, hi! Or if you're on what feels like night 128 of no sleep, or you've been walking for over an hour and *finally* have a sleeping bundle in the pram, yup, been there too. Welcome to motherhood.

When Peanut asked me to pen a few words about this book, I screamed with delight inside (and a little bit out loud too, to be honest). To be able to speak to any woman who is where I am, has been where I am or is going to be where I am, is an honour, and one I don't take it lightly. That's something my mum instilled in me. The fact that Peanut has been my saving grace on more sleepless nights and anxious mornings than I care to admit only makes it that bit more special. This book perfectly builds on what the Peanut community is: a place where we all come to learn, because we're all just figuring it out, and we're all in it together. Peanut knows that motherhood requires support, community, understanding, strength, love, forgiveness and, most importantly, other women who have lived it and have the battle scars to prove it – a village of them.

In those very early weeks of pregnancy, when only my partner and my GP knew I was pregnant, I had my village on Peanut to confide in, to ask whether it was normal, whether it would pass, whether salt and vinegar crisps had also become their main food group. When I was worrying whether my hair was really going to fall out after birth, or whether I was the only person in the entire world up at 3.23 a.m., rocking Billie to sleep, my village was there, telling me they were doing it too. A silent midnight army.

What I suppose I didn't really understand before becoming a mum is how strongly motherhood links you to other women. Something validating and almost magical happens when you hear another mum's experience of something, even when it's not the same as your own. Whatever our views or experiences, we have something that connects us. We were never really meant to raise children alone, so whether you're finding solace through the app or the pages of this book, know that you won't have to.

Chapter after chapter, I have lapped up the stories from real mums sharing real experiences about every stage of new motherhood. I was constantly nodding or folding down page corners to turn back to. Most importantly, I felt seen. So, when Peanut asked me to introduce you to this book, I thought about what I wanted you to know, what I wish someone had said to me when I was standing in your shoes. Above all, I want you to know that you are never alone in this. We are right there in the trenches with you, just a message away, just a few pages over. Because we're in this together. Consider me the first member of your village. You've got this.

Love, Rosie

Prologue

'Are you on the dating scene?'
'Have you met someone yet?'
'Are you going to get married?'

These are just the first in a long line of questions that women face throughout their lives. Society seems to have a map laid out for us: go to school, get a job, settle down and start a family. We memorize facts, study history, learn about the planets and discover that the mitochondria are in fact the powerhouse of the cell. Sixteen years of education packed with everything we'll need – except, you know, how to file a tax return or fix a leaky tap. And definitely nothing about the most important – and often overlooked – role many of us will step into: motherhood.

We leave school and move into the next phase of our meta-morphosis; many of us spend five years (or more) preparing for our dream futures and figuring out who we actually want to show up as in this world. We navigate our way through university, internships, sleepless nights, new friendships, office politics, broken hearts, promotions – all on the ascent to adulthood. Along the way, we're told we can do anything, be anything. We stand on the shoulders of the women before us, who fought for our right to education, equal pay and career opportunities. They shattered glass ceilings so we could take up our place in the world, with the message that women can have it all if we just work hard enough.

Then, without much warning, the questions change:

'Are you having a baby?'

'Are you having another one?'

'Are you going back to work?'

The stakes continue to rise. And everyone around us seems to know the path we should be on better than we do. For years, I pushed back against these questions. I told anyone who asked that I wasn't sure if I'd have kids. That I was too focused on my career. And part of that was true. I had spent years grinding away in the corporate world, convinced that reaching the top would define my success. Motherhood felt distant, something I'd think about later when I had ticked off more of my to-do list.

But motherhood didn't wait for me to be 'ready'. (What does ready even look like, anyway?) It didn't fit neatly into my carefully planned career trajectory. And it certainly didn't come with the instruction manual I desperately needed.

We don't talk about it — not in school, not in the workplace and certainly not in the self-help podcasts that tell us how to build a fulfilling career. Society presumes women will become mothers, but it forgets to hand us the toolkit on how to navigate that part of our lives. The result? We feel lost. We've prepared for everything else: our education, our careers — some of us are even spreadsheeting for our financial futures — but when it comes to motherhood, we're left fumbling in the dark.

I became a mother at the peak of my career, and in that moment, everything shifted. I felt fortunate and terrified at the same time. How could I step away from a role I loved? How could I pause a career I had worked so hard to build?

How could I be entirely responsible for this perfect little life form? The long and short of it is that I had no idea how to show up in the world as 'Michelle the mum', so I went back to work after five months, eager to prove that motherhood hadn't changed me. But the reality was, everything had changed.

I had been so focused on 'having it all' that I hadn't prepared for what that truly meant. I hadn't thought about how to balance motherhood with the rest of my life. I hadn't laid the groundwork for the emotional, physical and mental shift that comes with raising a child. And I didn't have the stories of other women – real women, with real struggles and real triumphs – to guide me.

Those are the things you look for in friends, but none of mine were in the same boat. Sure, in the early days with my son, Fin, some of my friends were also up at 3 a.m., but it was typically for a different kind of bottle service. Those were the moments in which I felt the loneliness the most. I'd gone from working a million miles an hour, constantly around people, to suddenly being at home all day on my own with this little dude. It was a difficult adjustment, and thanks to society (or stubbornness), I didn't feel like loneliness was something I could openly admit to. Because I *wasn't* alone: I had this baby and a loving family, and I swear I did have actual friends! I just didn't have anyone who *truly got it*. I needed people who understood what I was going through, or even better, were going through it themselves.

So, fast-forward through many, many sleepless nights, mum and baby classes and lonely sobs, to my realization that my experience in the world of tech and dating apps (and now, early motherhood) might actually propose a solution. I could modify the principles, algorithms and learnings to create a product that would help users connect with other like-minded women (who just so happened to be mamas). It was an idea born out of sheer necessity.

When the Peanut app progressed from idea to actual-thing-I'm-now-*actually*-doing, I had so many considerations in mind. I had only been a mum for a short time and was already sick of the way brands and products were addressing me, falling into outdated clichés and using othering terminology (I'm looking at you, 'DD2'). Seemingly the industry hadn't yet caught on to the fact that all mums are not the same. Not *all* of us are good at arts and crafts, and simply having kids isn't always enough in common to build a lasting friendship. I wanted to create opportunities for women to find friendships based on more than *just* this monumental, shared experience. You're allowed to have friends who like the same shows as you, or the same artist, or work in the same industry *and* who happen to be mums.

And now, that's exactly what over five million women around the world use Peanut for. We've created an online village where every unique mum can find her people, the answers to her questions, validation and support. We can pool information, have a laugh and be vulnerable together, knowing that we're in a safe space. I wanted it to be easy to find other mums who live close to you or whose kids are the same age or who also want to chat about the Kardashians when they're doing the night feeds. I wanted it to be easy to create authentic connections you can take offline and into a local cafe, and to access trustworthy expert-sourced information and advice. Basically, Peanut is a modern solution to a familiar problem: being a mother is hard work best carried out in a community, but too many of us have to do it in isolation.

In building Peanut, we've heard the stories and lived experiences of millions of women, and it's those experiences we've leaned on to bring you this book, along with expert insights from doctors, counsellors and therapists who are part of the Peanut network. We want it to be a trusted resource when you're deep in the thick of it and in need of support. To help you wade through tricky waters, like when you can somehow still remember Pythagoras' theorem but not for the life of you what day it is. It's the book I wish I had read in my twenties, before becoming a mother. It's for every new and expecting mother who is trying to navigate this incredible, overwhelming and beautiful journey without the village they thought would be there. It's for the women who want to know that they're not alone, that it's okay to feel uncertain, and that there's no one-size-fits-all approach to motherhood.

Because the truth is, the village may not look the way it used to, and it might not come flat-packed and ready for easy assembly, but that doesn't mean we can't build it ourselves from the ground up. Whether it's through friendships, online communities or simply sharing stories like the ones in this book, we can create our own support systems — ones that empower us to be the mothers — and the women — we want to be.

I am so grateful to every single woman who shared their stories with us to help bring this book to life. Like Peanut, it would not exist without the care, support and love that each and every one of you have brought to it. Whether you are a contributor who helped us to take the next step on connecting mothers around the world, or a reader about to discover the many unspoken but essential truths about motherhood, thank you for being a part of this journey. I feel so lucky to be a part of it with you.

Michelle Kennedy
Founder and CEO of Peanut

When I say motherhood is hard . . .

What I mean is, it's not motherhood, it's the mental load.
It's not the baby, it's the broken sleep,
It's not the lack of alone time, it's the lack of a village.
It's not matrescence, it's the not prioritizing maternal mental health,
It's not failing at breastfeeding, it's society's expectations failing me.
It's not the no days off, it's the no hands on.
It's not my postpartum body, it's the pressure to 'bounce back'.
Pregnancy glow to let herself go.
It's being over being undervalued.
I love being a mother, but motherhood is hard.
And maybe it could be easier.

– Jess Urlichs

Introduction

It's three in the morning. You're five days past your due date and you can't sleep because there is no such thing as a comfortable sleeping position any more. So you're wide awake and googling '100% safe ways to get labour started' with a mixture of nerves and excitement.

Fast-forward five weeks. It's three in the morning and the baby is wide awake, which means you're awake – trying to get them back to sleep. Maybe you're pacing in your kitchen, soothing them as they cry. Maybe you're propped up in bed, trying to feed them without waking your partner. Maybe you're slumped on the sofa for the fourth time tonight, because your baby is deep into cluster feeding and it's impossible to break the pattern of constant night feeds. You're beyond tired.

You catch yourself looking out the darkened window, wondering when it will get easier. You feel utterly alone, which is crazy, right? You have your baby right here after all those months or even years of waiting for them, and they're so perfect, so precious. There must be other mums out there, staring out their living-room window or pacing their kitchen, but at this precise moment you feel like the loneliest person in the world.

I've always wanted to be a mom but it's a lot of work, not just caring for them but also nurturing my sense of self. You don't have the time, energy, or mental capacity. And it can be very lonely.

— Stephanie W., US

Ask anyone who has ever had a child what it was like in the first few months and they're likely to get a haunted look in their eyes as they tell you about night feeds and colic, endless exploding nappies and mysterious rashes. The tiredness, confusion and worry mixed in with the sheer joy and wonder of suddenly having a tiny, infinitely precious human to love and care for. Life has been rearranged and will never be the same again. 'Nothing can prepare you for it,' they might say.

At Peanut, we're the first to admit that this is kind of true. Becoming a mother has a profound impact on every area of life, from your body to your relationships and even your sense of self. The changes are huge but, of course, they're also different for everyone. There's no such thing as the right way to be a mother because every mother is uniquely herself, caring for her unique child. How can you know what your particular struggles will look like until you're living them? There could never be a plan for motherhood, let alone a manual, because one size definitely does not fit all.

But while that's true, we also know for certain that sharing stories with people going through something similar, being connected to other mums, asking for tips, offering reassurance and sympathy and having a giggle at the craziness of it all can mean the difference between dreading each day and learning how to thrive in your new life.

Having mum friends makes being a mum a little easier, and easier is good — essential, actually — because while being

8

a mother is the most important role we'll ever have, it's also the toughest. The responsibility is so huge, it's practically guaranteed to feel overwhelming. What if we get something wrong? What if we get *everything* wrong? There's no time off, no respite. If we carried and birthed our baby, then our body has just gone through a profound transformation. Even if it all went fine, we're bound to be reeling. And for those of us whose childbirth was a struggle (or worse), we've got a lot of healing to do.

Whatever our route to motherhood – through adoption, surrogacy or pregnancy (assisted or not) – once the baby arrives, we're into new territory. A lot of it will be full of love and joy on a scale we've never known, but after a few months of sleep deprivation and all-day-every-day challenges, we're also likely to find ourselves feeling lonely, sad, confused, angry or anxious at three in the morning. How could we not?

This is a book about mothers, not children.

You'll lose your past self, and that will hurt. It might even feel as if you're completely disappearing. But if you can embrace this new role, you will be reborn – empowered and ready for the challenge.

— Fanny L., Mexico

Working out what's going to make your experience of motherhood as enjoyable as possible is no easy task because, as we know and you know, this stuff is highly personal and changing all the time. It's messy and emotional. It's stressful. There's still so much pressure to be that perfect mother who makes it all look easy: in tune with her children's needs while also being a great wife / girlfriend / lover / daughter / friend /

boss / colleague / cook / cleaner / taxi driver and picker-up of every single piece of Lego on the living-room rug.

So women research and make plans. We hoover up the endless stream of information about babies, parenting and what to expect when you're expecting. Books, blogs, posts, your doctor's opinion, your mum's opinion, your best friend's opinion. We're desperate to make sure we're equipped to give our child everything they need. And that's great; it's high up there in the job description of being a mum.

But there are so many other, less visible challenges, many of which are rooted in our needs rather than our child's. How do we make sure we have at least some time we can call our own? To heal, read, think, go to the gym, or just have a bloody shower? How should we be with our partner now we're parents? Where did all our friends go? Where can we find new ones who get this – and us? How do we go back to a job we love without feeling guilty and overstretched? How do we accept making some sacrifices now while ensuring we don't make sacrifices for ever? How do we feel sexy and sexual again? How do we make space for our own fun, as well as our child's? How do we feel seen, valued, appreciated, whole, whether we had our baby last week or five years ago?

These are the kinds of challenges that so many of us haven't given much thought to, until the day (or more likely the long sleepless night) when we realize, 'Wait a minute, I have questions. And I'm not sure I can google the answer.' You'll find much less information about a mother's struggles than you will about weaning, tantrums and all the rest, especially if you want accessible, verifiable information and honest opinions from the people who are actually living the same challenge. Mums' needs get overlooked. We overlook them ourselves.

My partner and I agreed that we wouldn't let starting a family change us and we'd keep everything exactly the same. It went the absolute opposite direction. We had to re-evaluate our whole relationship and almost start anew.
— **Brianne P.-L., US**

Realizing that we need help can make us feel really vulnerable. That's when every mum needs a village – not just to look after her baby (though another pair of hands to sterilize a few bottles wouldn't go amiss) but to help her figure this stuff out. To look after *her*. Mums need shoulders to cry on, cheerleaders, wise elders. We need expert advice on everything from setting boundaries with older relatives to post-partum sex. We need fresh perspectives, from people who've been there, mopped up the projectile bodily fluids and have the battle scars to prove it. Mums need a break, some understanding, and each other.

That's why Peanut was born, and that's precisely what this book sets out to give you. This isn't a parenting manual or a guide to baby and toddler development. There are countless great books on those subjects already. This is a book about *you*: your struggles, your joys and your discoveries. It's about how motherhood intersects with every other aspect of your life.

It doesn't push the idea that early motherhood is nothing but a slog. We know that many mums feel the pendulum has swung too far towards that story. They long to share their delight in motherhood and their joy in their kids but worry it won't be well received or will make other women who are struggling feel worse. The truth is that being a mum means life is extreme: it's both the best *and* the toughest role. Motherhood will give you the most uplifting moments you've ever experienced *and* take you right down to the depths. Your kids will drive you crazy *and* make your heart feel as if it's bursting with pure, joyous love. Mothers aren't convinced when the messages they're given about motherhood are too bland, too sentimental or too sensationalist. Being a mum is too multifaceted and mums are too complex to be satisfied with anything one-dimensional. Honesty is key. And that's what we've tried to deliver in the book. Above all, it covers the questions and issues that we've seen coming up over and over again, that mums like you bring to Peanut in search of information and reassurance.

We've arranged these questions roughly in the order that you might experience them, so for example, worries about birth come before 'How am I supposed to have a shower when my baby never sleeps?' 'Help, I can't find any mum friends' comes before 'Hold on, I have to go back to work and I'm not sure I'm ready.' But of course every mum is different and, although there are common themes, we're certainly not saying that this is how things go for everyone.

Some of us are tackling parenthood solo while others have a live-in partner. Some of our partners are a huge support – but some of them really aren't. Not everyone has their origin family living in the same town or even the same country. Some of us are estranged from family. Maybe we're closer to our in-laws, or maybe our in-laws are a pain in the arse. Maybe we have a social circle that flexes as children are born, maybe we don't. We might be working full-time, working part-time, staying at home with our kids or going back to school. We might be feeling stretched for cash or life might be relatively comfortable. So if there's a section about an issue that isn't relevant in your life, such as conflicts with a live-in partner when you're a single parent, feel free to skip right ahead (or if you prefer, dig in to hear how other mamas are feeling). Our circumstances and needs are different, but we can still learn from and support one another to find the most rewarding way through motherhood, for *us*.

Throughout the book you'll also find a number of 'sticky' topics. These are the ones that might cause friction between two camps at a mother and baby class, for example, or cause you to feel complex emotions months or even years down the line. It's not our intention to make a case for or against, just to lay out the issue and let you hear from other women who've been there and tackled the fallout. Seeing both sides of the story will, hopefully, make you feel more equipped to handle these debates, if and when they pop up. And – largely – hearing the point of view of other mums helps bridge the gap between camps, helping us all to understand each other a little better.

We've asked thousands of members of the Peanut community to tell us their stories and share their hard-won lessons on how to thrive as a mum. No matter the issue you're facing, the Peanut community has got your back. If you're finding it hard to adjust to this new aspect of your identity or you're looking for reassurance that you're not going mad – these mums are here for you. This book is a labour of love with hundreds of authors, and all of them have been where you are now.

> *I will always put my daughter first no matter what. But in order for me to do that and be the best I can, I have to take care of myself too.*
>
> **— Vanessa R., US**

It Takes a Village, like Peanut before it, was born out of our belief that every single mother deserves to feel secure, nurtured and seen within their community. We all need support networks that look after us as well as our children.

We also need and deserve to be our glorious whole selves, at every single stage of motherhood, so that we can really show up for our children. Aisling M., who lives in Spain, said, 'I didn't expect to feel so fiercely that my role is to hold space so that my daughter can grow into herself. I would do anything to help her be who she is. So I guess I have to lead by example and be unapologetically me!' Too right, Aisling.

We hope the stories collected in this book reassure you that you're not the only one struggling and help you see that, actually, you're doing a great job. We hope they inspire you to explore your village, reach out to ask for and offer help and, above all, enjoy this unique and precious time in your life as much as you possibly can. You and your children deserve nothing less.

Love,
Team Peanut

CHAPTER 1
Village, what village?

Let's get something straight, right from the start. It's not your fault if you're finding the stresses and strains of pregnancy and early motherhood tough. If you're feeling lonely and overwhelmed and are telling yourself that it's because of something you did or didn't do, please stop. Give yourself a break. Struggling with the adjustment to motherhood does *not* mean that you're failing as a mother. We know from listening to millions of women over the last few years that practically everyone has a voice in their head telling them that if only they were stronger, more resilient, laid-back or loveable, *different* in some way, then they would be gliding through life and loving every second of being a mum. They'd be tapping into their 'natural instincts' and getting everything right, from breastfeeding to potty training, while keeping on top of their life goals and their relationships, surrounded by supportive family and friends. And if that charming picture doesn't fit? If they're flailing rather than gliding? Then the little voice in their head chips in: *Bringing up a baby isn't rocket science. Everyone else can do it. You're not working hard enough. In fact, you're just not good enough.*

We are here to tell you, once and for all, that that voice is talking rubbish. You're absolutely good enough. If you're struggling, that's because it's hard. If you feel lonely, that's because being on your own with a baby all day is a crazy-making way to spend your time. If you long for help and support and company and reassurance, that's fair enough. You were never meant to do this job without the support of your village.

Morgan found this out for herself after she had her first child. She's 38, a therapist and mother of two who lives in Oklahoma City, US. She's bold and witty in conversation, despite being every bit as exhausted as you would expect of someone who has a toddler and a six-week-old baby. She speaks passionately about her work as a trauma therapist, and places a high value on honesty, transparency and vulnerability in all her relationships. She doesn't hesitate when asked for the most surprising thing she's learned about motherhood.

'You need to find a community of people because you can't do this job alone. You're going to need friends who drop by and say things like, "I was making bagels so I made you a set too." You need someone who will take your child when you feel sick at their house, lay you down on their couch and let you sleep. You need people you can call when you're crying. You need a rich and diverse community. I'm not talking about being a single parent versus having a partner. I'm talking about dis-covering that no individual mom, no individual family can do it alone. You need to find your village. And if the village doesn't exist, you have to build it. It may feel daunting but just start where you are, seek out one other person and look for ways to connect with more. It's worth it. I'm on good terms with the family I was born into but some of the structures I grew up with were not healthy. Same goes for my husband. My big question is, how do I provide the secure, loving, open-hearted environment that I didn't have when I was growing up? That's what I need to figure out, and I know I can't do it alone.'

Morgan wanted a lot more support than she'd anticipated, and she struggled to find it. This was the aspect of motherhood that really caught her out. 'Motherhood is a wild ride,' she said. 'When it's hard, it's really hard, but when it's great, it's *so* great, and you can swing between those extremes several times every hour. It's a complex job, and we tend to blame ourselves when it's hard.' Morgan, like millions of other women, arrived at Peanut feeling scared that she was the only one struggling, only to discover that she was in great company. She began to open up with other mums and ask for help as well as offer it.

So why do women like Morgan end up feeling caught out? Why do so many of us discover too late that raising a child without losing ourselves is too important a task for one person or even one set of parents? If it's obvious to mothers that they need a village, why is it so hard to find one? Was it always like this? What happened? There are lots of answers to these big questions, but our individual failure is not one of them. It's society that fails mothers, by telling us that we have a duty to be perfect all the time and then denying us adequate family leave, affordable childcare and healthcare, secure housing and social support, not to mention genuine respect and value for the work we do.

Loneliness is another big problem. The ideal of the nuclear family – mum, dad and kids shut away in their own house – can lead to isolation. Single mothers, and young mothers whose peers are on a different life track, can feel particularly alone with their children. Many of us end up living far away from our family of origin and the friends we grew up with. If we have a baby with someone from another state or country, potential isolation is baked into our experience of family life.

Women shifting into motherhood are vulnerable, whatever

our circumstances, and yet we're routinely expected to figure it all out, and then we're ignored or shamed if we voice any ambivalence or distress. This reflects a bigger truth about the way our society often treats vulnerable and marginalized people – by making them feel that it's their fault if they're not coping, when in reality they're up against a systemic crisis that's bigger than they are. That's part of the reason why we all need a village. But the other reason is that motherhood is just more fun when you have a supportive crew to giggle and commiserate with.

Pregnant women and new mothers sense this and identify with the idea of a village. When we asked Peanut users if they'd heard the saying 'It takes a village to raise a child', more than 97 per cent of them told us they had. It's found in slightly different versions in many African languages, including Runyoro, which is spoken in Uganda; Haya, spoken in Tanzania; and Swahili, spoken across east Africa. It's been well known outside of the region at least since Hillary Clinton used it back in the 1990s. How and why did this proverb take on such a life of its own that it became a staple in the English language? Perhaps because of what it says to us. It offers a time-poor, emotionally stretched mother some reassurance that if she is struggling, it might be because she doesn't have the backup she needs – not because she's not up to the job. That's a powerfully comforting idea. It also serves as rocket fuel for women's determination to demand more for themselves and their children. No wonder mums remember this phrase. When they, like Morgan, discover how hard motherhood can be, it has the potential to steer them away from self-blame and in search of solutions.

One mum described her ideal village as: 'A mixture of family, friends, mentors, neighbours, people who you respect and love and who want to see you succeed. A group you bring together that feels nourishing and nurturing.' Another summed it up simply and powerfully as: 'A community that sticks together to support each other along this journey of parenthood.' But when we asked whether women felt part of such a village, fewer than half said yes. Many mums felt their village was too small to be a reliable support. Most people, 72 per cent to be precise, said they depended on immediate family. Friends were mentioned by 23 per cent of respondents. Only 13 per cent said they counted on extended family, and less than 1 per cent of people thought of educators, health professionals, neighbours, mentors or the wider community. It seems there is a big gap between what women hope for – a network of people who can lend a hand in many different ways – and their lived reality.

It is crazy how quickly you realize you don't have a village. I moved towns just before my daughter was born, so I wasn't expecting to see my family as much, but they hardly make any time for me, and they expect a lot. It can be really, really lonely out here in motherhood!
— Emily V., UK

Motherhood is 'a uniquely tough gig'

In *Eve*, a bestselling book about female biology and evolution published in 2023, the science writer Cat Bohannon talks about human childhood as being 'a uniquely tough gig' from the mother's point of view. Birthing a baby with a disproportionately large head through a comparatively narrow pelvis is no picnic, for a start. Compared to a newborn chimp, which can walk after only four weeks, a human newborn is fantastically needy, requiring an adult caregiver to do everything, for *years*. Human beings have a long childhood, during which the brain rewires itself at super speed as we learn how to be social, how to communicate and how to get stronger and more independent – so long as *someone* is teaching us how. In other words, human babies are really hard work. They always have been.

In the past, most societies recognized this. The care of young children was carried out by a group, often of women from different generations but sometimes a mixed group of kinfolk. That meant wisdom could be passed on, lived experience could be channelled and an exhausted mother could catch a nap from time to time. Some cultures still operate on this basis, but many do not. Most of us having babies in countries like the States, Canada, Australia and the UK don't witness the reality of pregnancy, birth and early mothering until we're in it. We are encouraged to think of motherhood as something we can do relatively easily, so long as we get the right products and relax into our natural role.

Claudia Tomalino, who is from Italy but lives in Cambridge, UK, with her husband and their 15-month-old daughter, thinks that she underestimated the challenge partly because of these cultural narratives. She describes her attitude as a little naive. 'I've always been very independent, but even so, what was I thinking? Then again, maybe as a culture we don't talk about what it's really like to have children. Our stories are not completely honest. And we are told that if you can't cope, there's something wrong with you.' Contrast this story with the idea of the village that steps in to help. In *that* story there is a recognition that the job is hard, and much easier and more fun when carried out in a community.

Tola Awe-Cunningham is a mother and grandmother living in Bradford, UK. She was born in the UK to a British mother and Nigerian father, but at the age of four, went to live with her father's family just outside Lagos, where she spent her childhood and adolescence and eventually became a mother herself. Her experience reflects the values and approach encapsulated in the proverb: it takes a village to raise a child.

'In Nigeria, I was used to a culture of unconditional love and support. I grew up near Lagos in a town called Ibadan, in a house full of family. I was raised by my aunt, Moni Bankole, whom I call "mummy". My grandmother lived in my father's hometown of Ilesha and often visited. There were always at least ten people in the house and many more coming and going. Every weekend there was a reason to celebrate with prayers, food, music and dancing.'

Tola brought up her sons as she had been brought up herself, in an extended family who looked out for her boys, told them off if necessary and gave them a cuddle when they needed one. 'Being a mother was embedded in community. I didn't know any different. If you needed help with your children, you only had to ask. It wasn't planned ahead of time. I would say to my neighbours, "Could you look after my boys while I go to the shop?" The reply was, "Of course." It worked both ways. I often looked after other women's children. It meant my boys had playmates, so it was good for the children as well as the adults.'

Tola was 28 when she moved back to Britain. She settled near her mum in Yorkshire and has been there ever since. She brought her sons a year later, once she had secured a job and somewhere to live; the eldest was six, the second was three, and the youngest just one. 'Adjusting to life in Bradford was tough for all of us. The hardest thing was the different culture.

Everyone was much more reserved. Very polite but also very concerned to mind their own business. I didn't know how to be that way. I had to learn how to ask for what I needed in the British way and then teach my boys to do the same. I missed the support network terribly, especially when I was studying to be a chartered accountant at the same time as working. The presence of more family and neighbours would have been priceless. It wasn't until years later that I realized I had depression during my first few years in the UK.'

Tola acknowledges that while she found the typical British approach too insular, nothing and nowhere is perfect. 'Sometimes the family and the gatherings could be almost too much in Nigeria. People were very nosy – though people are nosy everywhere.' She has long since adjusted to the realities of contemporary British family life. 'I don't live in the same city as one grandchild or the same country as the other, so I travel a lot. I fit round my sons' family schedules and preferences. It isn't the way I would have chosen but I understand it is the way life is, when love directs.'

Tola's experience shows us how the village steps in to help with children as part of a wider community life that includes activities like worship, eating and dancing together. It also flags up that the traditional 'takes a village' approach won't work in different places and times without being adapted to our specific local culture and situation.

Plenty of mums told us how they and their families were making these adaptations. Mitra is of Indian heritage and lives in London. When she gave birth to her first child in March 2020, her mum came over from New Zealand to look after her, enabling Mitra to focus on caring for her baby. 'It's relatively normal in South Asian cultures for a woman's mother to come and stay when she gives birth. The new mother requires so much care during those first few weeks and we take the view that the grandmother is supporting her to make the transition. I focused on feeding my baby, as my mother focused on feeding me.'

Anessa is from Pittsburgh and lives in Montreal with her husband, who's from Ghana, and their son. Female members of her husband's family came to stay with her for three months after she gave birth. 'I barely had to get out of bed for weeks,' Anessa told us. 'All my food was cooked for me. I was told that I needed to rest and recover, and that was great. It hasn't always been easy, though. There are a lot of people with a lot of opinions. But my husband supports me to hold boundaries. He understands that I have different values.'

Not everyone wants to bring up their children with lots of other voices chipping in, of course, or to live in the same house as their in-laws. Anessa echoed Tola's comments that sometimes the village feels intrusive, though she also underlined that the support was invaluable, especially in the first few weeks and months of her child's life. But the reality for most of us is that we don't have multi-generational family support on our doorstep. We're less likely than ever to live in communities where several adults feel invested in helping out with child-rearing.

Not all of us are emotionally close to the family in which we grew up, even if they do live round the corner. Some of us wouldn't want to be in the same room with them, let alone have them involved in caring for our children. Some family dynamics are toxic, and many women consider it their life's mission to break generational patterns – to parent vastly differently from the way they were parented themselves. Other mums have lost one or both parents in younger life and are navigating motherhood while grieving again for the parents who have died. Whatever our circumstances, many of us are heading into motherhood without the backup of our elders.

If modern motherhood has changed, so too has modern fatherhood. Dads often play a much bigger role in the early life of their children than they did 30 or 40 years ago, and this can make a huge positive difference to women's experience of motherhood. But many women find themselves up against uncomfortable realizations about gender roles when they and their partner become parents. In 2023, Peanut published a report titled *Invisible Mothers* on the unseen struggles and unacknowledged labour performed by mothers. Of those we questioned, 71 per cent said that a more equal division of parenting tasks with their partner would make being a mother easier, and we hear countless stories of resentment over the mental and emotional load that mothers overwhelmingly carry.

Besides, not every child comes with a father attached. Some women, such as Marcia from Philadelphia, US, and her wife, opt to become parents by using an anonymous sperm donor. Some women are single parents when they hadn't expected to be, due to the breakdown of the relationship with their child's father. Others are choosing to parent solo right from the start. Some are creating families with friends, or blended families with new partners, adding the role of stepparent to every other hat they're wearing. The bottom line is, once we're a mother, our intimate relationships get more complex than ever before.

Beyond families and partners, loneliness is an issue for many of us even before we have a baby. Feeling overstressed and under-connected with friends, neighbours and community is a feature of modern life. Many of us get by okay until the day we realize we're feeling vulnerable and we don't have anyone to ask for help. It could be that we get sick, or we lose our job, or have a life crisis, or *we have a child*. And then we think, where is my village when I need it? If we have the resources, we might hire a childminder or pay for some therapy, depending on how we're struggling. But when costs are soaring, paying for the help we need isn't always an option. We need a network of loose connections that provide mutual aid – the neighbours who can look after our toddler while we run to the shop, knowing we will do the same for them, as was normal for Tola. And many of us don't have it.

As Jess Urlichs puts it so brilliantly in her poem, featured at the start of this book, motherhood is hard in unexpected ways. It's not the being with our children that makes mother-hood feel so draining for many of us. (Sure, we're tired; but we expected that and besides, they're at least as joyous and hilarious as they are tiring.) It's the endless tasks – physical, mental and emotional – that surround it. It's the isolation and the loneliness. It's the lack of sincere appreciation or value for the caring work we do. The lack of respect and support.

That lack of support can be systemic – the absence of adequate statutory maternity leave or affordable nursery care – and it can be specific to your particular circumstances – maybe you've just moved house and you're in a new city where you know nobody, with a toddler who needs friends just as much as you do. Maybe you've just kicked your baby's dad out because enough is enough. Whatever the situation, feeling like you're not able to be the mother that you long to be always sucks.

We see you. Please know that you're not the only one who feels like this. Our *Invisible Mothers* report showed that an alarming 93 per cent of mothers regularly feel unacknow-ledged or unseen in their role as a mother. And the worst culprits, interestingly, are friends and family. The very same groups that the majority of us depend on most heavily for support. Of those we asked, 58 per cent said they felt unappreciated by their friends and 57 per cent by family. Almost three out of every five mothers are frustrated with the only people they feel they have around them as a source of potential support. Something has *clearly* gone wrong with our village.

None of this is your fault

The gap between the village a mother craves and her lived reality can add an extra layer of stress to her struggle. Where are her people and why is this so hard? Was it something she did, something she said? The self-doubting questions about what it means to be 'a good mother' kick in well before we've even given birth to our child. Veronica Cisneros is a US-based licensed marriage and family therapist who specializes in helping women navigate motherhood and careers while looking after themselves. She's one of the Peanut Professionals, expert members of our community whose specialist knowledge we will be drawing on throughout the book. Veronica has worked with hundreds of mothers and knows all about the insecurities many of us are dealing with. 'The minute you're pregnant, you instantly feel like you're doing everything wrong and you can't win. *I'm not eating enough. I'm eating too much.* It doesn't stop. You end up with a world of doubt and comparison, and that can lead to insecurity. It feels as if everyone else knows what they're doing and you're the only one struggling, when of course the absolute opposite is true.'

Time and again mums tell us that they're worried they're not doing motherhood 'right'. It's as if it's not enough to be a good mother for your child. You also need to be the right kind of mother for your family, or your social circle. You need to be the right kind of mother on social media. So many women compare themselves to others, while undervaluing their own experiences. In the sometimes competitive and always slightly anxious world of early motherhood, our worries can get out of hand if we don't have people we can share them with honestly.

Whatever our particular issues, lack of reliable support makes them feel so much harder. The emotional toll on women is huge. Anxiety is the norm among our community, with 86 per cent of women experiencing it. Stress is a problem for 82 per cent of mothers, as is burnout. Loneliness and overwhelm are mentioned by 80 per cent of women and irritability by 78 per cent. That's a potent cocktail of unhappiness affecting the vast majority of mums.

For some of us, the anxiety and resentment become overwhelming. Sometimes that makes us tired and sad. Sometimes it messes up our self-esteem, other times it undermines our relationships. It can even affect whether we have more children. Katarina from the US told us, 'I very naively romanticized the idea of motherhood. Having my third has shown us how non-existent our village is. We actually want more children but feel we do not have the help we need for our family as it is.'

It's clear that in practice, most women's network is restricted to a tight group of close friends and immediate family, who may not be that supportive. Extending that network or working on those existing relationships takes effort. And how much effort can a mum make when she's dealing with the last stage of a challenging pregnancy, is worried about her baby's development or is sleep-deprived and coming to terms with the unexpected shock of motherhood?

That last one is the missing piece of the puzzle that makes everything else harder. Everyone who's about to have a baby knows they're going to be tired and they'll be clearing up a lot of poop. Women know that raising a child is hard work, and in the early years it's draining, repetitive work. What we *don't* know, because nobody tells us, is that raising ourselves as mothers is also work. We have to learn so many new skills and take on so many new roles. We need to grow into motherhood just as we help our child to grow into being themselves. A little guidance and a little company wouldn't go amiss.

Maybe we need a new version of the proverb. Sure, it takes a village to raise a child. It also takes a village to raise a mother.

When a baby is born, so is a mother

We followed up our questions about the 'village to raise a child' proverb by asking the Peanut community whether they had heard of 'matrescence'. This term refers to the idea, which is gaining traction in scientific circles, that becoming a mother is a biological and emotional process that extends well beyond pregnancy and even the fourth trimester. Only 6 per cent of people had heard of it but it seems that plenty more grasped its significance. One admitted, 'I hadn't heard of the term until googling it but now I can say it has been the most challenging stage of my life.'

In her book *Matrescence: On the Metamorphosis of Pregnancy, Childbirth and Motherhood*, Lucy Jones explores the scientific evidence that women's brains and hormones change so much during this time that it should be considered a unique, bio-logically distinct stage of life. If adolescence describes the period of physical, emotional and social changes that we undergo during puberty, matrescence is the equivalent for people who are pregnant and postpartum. And just as teen-agers have a lot to learn, so do new mothers. Teens are preparing for independent life, and their brains and bodies are going through a potentially rough adjustment while they learn the new skills they'll need. Mums are going through something very similar: hormones, neurology, physical health, mental health, emotions and identity – everything is shifting because our life has just changed radically. We've got a new role and a whole lot of learning to do . . .

The difference is that while teenagers are understood to be passing through a difficult transition and are, to a greater or lesser degree, cut some slack by society, new mothers are rarely afforded the same understanding. We're expected to take the shifts in our stride, buoyed up by our supposedly 'natural instincts' for mothering and caregiving. The traditional ideal of motherhood requires us to focus all our attention and energy on our baby and simply adapt gracefully to our new life. Which describes the experience for some women, but not for most. New motherhood is often messier and more sensi-tive than that, more visceral and more challenging.

Lucy Jones makes the case that many difficulties stem from biological changes that help a new mum adapt to her care-giving role but have gone too far and tipped into unhelp-ful territory. So, for example, the intrusive negative thoughts that many women report in the first few months might be linked to changes in the brain that increase their sensitivity to threat. A new mum's brain has evolved to be hypervigilant, which makes sense on one hand but really isn't helpful when it translates to feeling too anxious to leave the house with your baby. If you pile sleep deprivation and feeling lonely on top of these neurochemical changes, you're creating a perfect storm for women and their children.

This is all to say that if you're feeling isolated, under-appreciated, resentful, scared, anxious, disappointed or regret-ful, that's not because you're screwing up. It's because you're carrying out a really challenging task – raising a child, keeping them safe and teaching them about the world – at the same time as living with a body, brain and nervous system that have literally been rearranged by pregnancy and postpartum. And all without the backup that ideally you would have from your tribe, your kin or a properly funded healthcare and early-years support system. Basically, you're not wrong if you're realiz-ing that this motherhood business is way harder than you'd thought.

> *I like to send other mums a message once in a while –*
> *no pressure, just a check-in. I remember how much*
> *that would have meant to me when my first was a few*
> *months old.*
>
> **— Stephani E., US**

We are definitely not saying that being a new mum is all doom and gloom and struggle and sacrifice, but neither is it necessarily easy, natural or graceful. We know how important honesty is to our community. That means we're here for all your mothering moments: the tricky and the adorable, the heartbreaking and the hilarious. After all, being open about the hard stuff doesn't detract from your deep love for your children, or your delight in the small moments of everyday joy that make it all so absolutely worthwhile.

Mums who are further along the road of motherhood will often stress that it gets easier. Slowly, sometimes painfully, but it does. Which is fine as far as it goes but still daunting when you're wading through the postpartum trenches. That's the issue we wanted to tackle in this book. How can you find the reassurance, information and support you need while you're waiting for it to get easier? How can you raise yourself as a mother while also raising your kids? How can we create the support networks that will hold us and our families lightly but securely? How can we contribute to other women's sense of being supported on their journey? How can we build the village we need? And how can we do all that without burning out, losing ourselves or missing out on the joy of parenting our children?

In Peanut's fantasy world, we'd pass a law that all pregnant women and mothers would be entitled to decent maternity leave. They would live within ten minutes of at least one person who dropped in to visit them and their baby once a week minimum, and could be called at 3 a.m. in any emergency, from a hospital trip to a four-hour crying spell – yours or the baby's. We would all have access to a weekly minimum of two hours of me-time that didn't involve spending any money, and we would have health providers that treat us with respect. Our fantasy world is basically like the village on steroids, stuffed with sources of help, from the friend who makes you laugh no matter how tired you are to the wise elders who've seen it all before. In this world, mums are listened to, seen, acknowledged, celebrated and welcomed.

But we don't live in this ideal world just yet. Until we do, the Peanut community's stories show us the way to face this challenge: by asking for and offering help, without shame and without judgement, and with lots of compassion. It makes us feel vulnerable to ask for help, but our shared vulnerability is the basis of the village.

It will take time to find your village; it's not the kind of thing you can achieve in one focused session, which is lucky since focus is in short supply in early motherhood. Creating your village is made up of hundreds of small acts of kindness, bravery and vulnerability. It takes listening to yourself and to others. It's so much fun along the way, though. There will be giggles and gratitude, conflicts resolved and new self-knowledge.

We can all do this. We just have to refocus on connection, generosity, solidarity and openness to others. Slow down, pay attention, talk to people, listen. That way, we rebuild connections that will sustain us and our families. We weave the kind of network that Tola experienced in Lagos and Morgan is building with other mums in Oklahoma City. It won't look exactly the same in every community, of course, but as long as we centre ourselves on openness and kindness, we'll be giving ourselves and our children the best opportunity to thrive.

We hope you find one version of your village here, in the pages of this book, in the stories and experiences of other mothers. At the end of every chapter we'll pull together some key strategies based on observations from mums and the experts who work with our community – you might find they spark new ideas about your own situation. We're offering them as a set of things to think about rather than tips or hacks. (Motherhood is pretty resistant to life hacks, as we're sure you've noticed.) Here's a selection of things to think about, inspired by the idea of community.

In a nutshell . . .

Bring compassion for yourself and for other mums who are also doing their best in crazy times. Try not to put too much pressure on yourself, or leap to quick judgements. You deserve respect and kindness, so give it to yourself as well as to those you meet. And remember that while motherhood is of course important, it can feel good to take it a little less seriously. Laughing at our mistakes rather than judging them is an act of self-compassion and opens us up to laugh with other mamas.

Find your people. Authentic connections will feel more nourishing and are much easier to sustain. If at first you don't find mums you click with, or support you can rely on, try not to get disheartened. Keep looking until you find them. If you're on a specific side quest, like trying to alter generational patterns through your parenting, for example, seek out other mamas on the same journey and it will feel less like an uphill battle.

Check in with people. Look for light-touch ways to reach out. A text message or a simple 'hello' at a coffee shop can make all the difference to how connected you feel – and it's mutually beneficial. Even a sympathetic smile when someone's baby is crying can be enough to help that woman feel seen. And who knows, it might be the start of a beautiful friendship!

Think about what your village means to *you*. Our village is partly about shared efforts but also about shared experiences and values. What does *your* ideal village look like? What kinds of support do you crave? Try to get specific. That will make it easier to seek out the help you need.

PART ONE
The third trimester

CHAPTER 2

Does anyone ever feel ready for motherhood?

On having a plan, being prepared, feeling ready

Sophia Lee is 28 years old, and eight months pregnant with her first child. She lives with her partner in Kansas City, US. Sophia is softly-spoken and intensely thoughtful. She endured emotional manipulation and controlling behaviour from her mother when she was growing up, so for Sophia, preparing to be a mother is about confronting patterns of behaviour and setting boundaries to ensure that her son will not be exposed to the harmful dynamics she had to cope with.

'Using the time during my pregnancy to set boundaries with my mother was absolutely the most important thing for me. I knew it would be even harder once the baby came, so this was my best opportunity. Everything else was extra. Setting up the nursery, picking a name, the gender reveal . . . I didn't even think about any of it. I started to worry the moment I told my mom I was pregnant. In my community a grandson is very important. My mom immediately went to, *How can I use this baby to show off to my friends or put him in programs where it would benefit me?* I've explained very clearly what I will and won't tolerate. She's not going to be alone with my son, and what my partner and I say is absolutely the final word on how we bring up our child. She didn't react well initially, but the conversations have got easier and I'm hoping that she will learn how to behave differently around my child from the way she behaved around me.'

Do you (or did you) feel ready to become a mother? It's a big question, right? You might be thinking, *sort of*, or *yes definitely*, or *not even close*. After all, readiness looks very different to different people. Does it mean having your baby's crib set up and a freezer full of lasagne, or having difficult conversations with your controlling mother? For some of us it might mean planning how to share childcare with our live-in partner, for others it's about seeking out our single-mum village online. For you, it might mean drawing up a plan in case your mental health issues flare up, or just taking some mindful time every day to reflect on what's coming.

When we reached out to the Peanut community for their thoughts on being prepared and feeling ready for motherhood, many women told us about trying to anticipate the impact of parenthood on their lives. We heard about everything from writing detailed birth plans and carefully researching buggies and bassinets, to discussions with partners on issues from postpartum sex to postnatal depression.

Some women told us that they had felt ready for years, having always known they wanted to be mothers. Being prepared became more of a practical question. Did they have the kit they needed? Or perhaps a social one: would they meet potential mum friends at antenatal classes? Some said they had gradually moved into emotional readiness having achieved other dreams, whether that was focusing on their career, going travelling or prioritizing their own development. As Mitra from London put it, 'I was 37 when I had my first child. I'd lived a lot of life and I was ready for this phase.

Although, nothing could have prepared me for the physical onslaught of new parenthood. And ultimately, the nature of the job is that you have to learn it as you go along.'

Other women found their readiness when they learned they were going to become mothers. Many people told us moving stories about stepping firmly up to motherhood, fully conscious of wanting to be a different kind of parent and break the bonds of family trauma. People like Julia O. from the UK, who said, 'The day I saw two pink lines on the test, everything in my life changed. All I could think about was being there for my baby and making memories as a family. I didn't have a happy childhood or parents: that's why I promised to give it my all as a mum and be present for every milestone, every sleepless night, every family adventure.'

But not everyone wants to plan meticulously and not everyone has the chance to prepare. Where a pregnancy was unexpected, especially if it came early in a relationship, preparation was often rushed or sidelined. Jane H., from the UK, told us that she spent her pregnancy dealing with the breakdown of her relationship with the baby's father. Getting ready for birth was very much a solo struggle. 'We'd only been together for three months when I got pregnant. We didn't know each other well and I was love-bombed. We tried to make it work but I had to walk away so that I could actually prepare for motherhood.'

And plenty of women figured that since birth and motherhood are intrinsically unpredictable, a flexible mindset was their best approach. They preferred to follow their instincts as events unfolded, trusting that they would learn on the job. As Anastasia K., who lives in the States and has a three-month-old baby, told us, 'I got pregnant when I was 18 and unemployed. I definitely wasn't ready in one sense but it's made me realize how much I can learn. Before I had my son, I spent my whole life feeling very disposable. Becoming a parent made me realize I'm not.'

An extended journey to motherhood didn't necessarily translate to women feeling more prepared. Lots of women who underwent fertility treatment told us that they were far more focused on getting and staying pregnant than actually becoming a mother. Dr Zoya is another of the Peanut Professionals, a London-based doctor with a speciality in dermatology who runs her own clinic and has two-year-old twin girls. 'I wasn't prepared at all. Everything was a shock to me. I'd had multiple miscarriages and been on the IVF journey, so I couldn't quite believe it was actually going to happen until the consultant put the babies on my shoulders and I heard them cry.'

On the other hand, Joanna D., who lives in Sussex, UK, with her two adopted children, told us that she definitely felt both ready and prepared. 'I always knew I wanted to be a mother and that I would go down the adoption route. My husband and I had to undergo a long process of checks, trainings and supervision. It took years and it was pretty gruelling but it meant that we had to be very intentional about our values around parenting. We're on the same wavelength now because we were forced to have those conversations.'

I had worked in childcare, so I did have some frame of reference. I knew kids were a 24/7 responsibility. But there's no real way to prepare until you're in it. You can't realize the mental toll it takes until you experience it.

— Stephanie W., US

Get a plan, do your prep or seek your readiness – your way

It may sound obvious but it's easy to overlook the fact that there is no single right way to prepare for motherhood; there's only the way that feels right to you. If we're really honest, you might not figure out what that is until months or even years down the line. Which might be frustrating but is also super common. Motherhood is such a huge and personal experience that even trying to *describe* it can feel like wrestling an octopus into a string shopping bag. The octopus is slippery and shifting and impossible to control. The bag might be flexible and surprisingly strong but it's also full of holes that allow the octopus to spill out and try to wriggle away. How would you ever prepare for an experience like that? How could you possibly learn how to do it, except by trying? Perhaps being ready is less about certainty, a list or a plan and more about your attitude and mindset.

One thing we know for sure is that while motherhood is complex and ever-changing, that doesn't mean preparation is a waste of time. It can be empowering and useful to reflect on our strategies and think ahead a little – as long as we focus on what feels right for us, rather than what we think we *should* do or what everyone else seems to be doing. There really is no single correct way to prepare yourself for any aspect of motherhood.

For example, we asked women with partners whether they'd discussed ahead of time how becoming parents might impact their relationship. The results were pretty evenly split between those who had and those who hadn't. Around 56 per cent said they did chat with their partner about this before their first child was born; 44 per cent didn't.

Of those who discussed it, one in three said they were still taken aback by how much being parents changed things – and not in a good way. But some people were pleasantly surprised. 'One night when I was super pregnant, I ended up in tears, saying to my partner that we'd never cuddle in bed ever again. The reality is better than I feared.' Or: 'We talked a lot about not romanticizing having a baby and then being deflated by its impacts. Actually, it wasn't as difficult as we thought it would be. There were hard times but they didn't last long. We got through them together.' And whether they were pleasantly or unpleasantly surprised, a clear majority of those who talked about how they would parent together felt that the conversation had been useful.

What was striking was that *not* discussing parenting with your partner ahead of time didn't necessarily mean bad outcomes. Some people in that group did say they wished they'd talked about it, but plenty of others said things like, 'I don't remember discussing it. I don't think we really had any clue what was coming but I feel we have both embraced it.' It seems that if you're a go-with-the-flow kind of couple, used to communicating and learning together, you'll probably be fine without detailed planning in advance.

So perhaps the lesson here is that planners like to plan, the free-flow crew will flow freely and there's a limit to how much any of us can prepare for motherhood. Approach the question of readiness with an open mind and tackle it from your own angle, knowing that whether you prep, plan or float your way towards meeting your baby, there are bound to be some surprises coming your way.

Claudia Tomalino said something interesting about this.

'Before becoming a parent I felt very positive about it. My partner was worried about how it might affect us, which is why he originally didn't want a child. We've both confirmed our expectations: he is finding it terribly hard, I am finding it an amazing experience. But we have also found something we didn't anticipate: I didn't expect to need so much help. My partner did not expect to fall in love with our daughter in the way he has.'

> My husband and I talked about parenting before our son was born and I thought we were both on the same page. The reality is, he's a helicopter parent and I'm closer to Montessori. We're finding our way now, but I really wasn't expecting that!
>
> — Danielle M., US

What might useful preparation look like?

As we've seen, some women, like Sophia, had difficult but necessary conversations with family about boundaries, behaviour and expectations. Others, like Jordan Shane, who is five months pregnant, carried out research into every single product they would need and planned every practical question meticulously. 'Due to my anxiety I have to have everything planned, bought and ready to go. I'm still three months off giving birth but my hospital bag and diaper bag are already packed.'

Many mums who struggle with their mental health react in this way, but it's by no means confined to women with a history of anxiety. For all of us who are planners, it can feel deeply reassuring to make a list and do our research, pack a bag and prepare the newborn essentials. The nesting instinct is a very real thing and it can help us to feel safe and secure as we face up to the deep uncertainty of parenthood.

If you have any extra challenges, it makes even more sense to want to prepare in specific, often practical ways. Perhaps you're a single mum who will be reliant on hands-on support in the first few weeks. Maybe your partner is going straight back to work, or you're expecting multiples. Some situations demand a little more structure. If that's the case for you, it's probably going to help you feel calmer if you consider how you'll manage your daily routine. Dr Zoya told us: 'Drawing up a rough schedule ahead of time was important to us because we had two babies coming, so we couldn't just wing it, we needed to know who was doing which tasks when. We had a rota for feeds, baths, bottle washing, the whole thing. That felt helpful and I'm glad we did it, but I wish I'd thought more about the support network we would need. You know, finding all the people you can for your bubble, opening your arms to the village – it's so important.'

Dr Zoya's words of wisdom really hit home for us. If there's one thing that we know to be true, because we hear it time after time from mums in every set of circumstances and from all over the world, it's the value of thinking ahead about your social networks and the kinds of support you might need. 'I would suggest prepping your supporters in advance,' said Dr Zoya. 'Be honest. Obviously, you can't know for sure exactly how things will go but it can remove a lot of stress to say to your family or friends, "These are the three to six months when we're really going to need practical support. Are you up for that?" It's always better to know about people's capacity. And it helps to minimize any disappointment and conflict later if you can discuss it ahead of time.'

Prepare mentally as much as you can before you have your children. Be ready to learn to adapt. And communicate, communicate, communicate – with your partner, family, friends, everyone!

— Caroline C., UK

Finally, remember that you can totally do this. Yes, it's a big job. Yes, it's slightly crazy that we get sent home from the hospital with a newborn, or wave goodbye to the midwife after our home birth, and the world trusts us to just . . . get on with it. There will be challenges and there are definitely downsides to being left to figure it all out – nobody knows that better than us. But we also know that mums are amazing. *You* are amazing. It's time to believe in yourself.

In a nutshell . . .

There's no 'right' way to prepare for motherhood. If you're a planner and it makes you feel good to plan, do it. Write those lists, tick off those purchases. If you're a little more 'go with the flow', don't stress yourself out by thinking of this phase of your life as a to-do list.

Thinking it through can help you feel positive. Remember that, ultimately, the goal of any preparation is to make life feel easier, support your mental health and boost your mood. Set a clear intention that you will only plan, reflect, think and discuss with that goal in mind.

Social connections matter more than buying kit. If you do nothing else, have a think about who you'll be talking to and hanging out with over the next few months. Whether that means approaching family for help in the first few weeks or seeding friendships with other pregnant women in your area, anything you can do is almost certain to be time and energy well spent.

You've got this! Know that whatever your circumstances, you are more resilient, creative and capable than you can imagine. Motherhood is not like taking an exam – you can't pass or fail. It's a relationship, with your child and your new self. Try to stay open-minded, curious and kind – especially to yourself.

CHAPTER 3

Is everything okay?

On health worries and roller coaster emotions

How are you feeling? Are you glowing or grouchy as you approach your due date? Maybe a bit of both, depending on how much your back aches this morning and how stressed you are about that upcoming appointment with your doctor. If you're working right up until the end, you might be too busy to think about anything except getting through the day. And if this is your second or a subsequent child, you're already juggling someone else's needs alongside your own. Pregnancy has to fit in around all your other responsibilities and activities.

Jordan Shane is 27 years old and lives with her partner in Vancouver, Washington. She's five months pregnant with their first child. Jordan has diagnoses of ADHD and anxiety and is open about the challenges of coping with her fluctuating emotions and mental health during pregnancy. She is also kick-ass smart (literally – she works as a martial arts instructor), funny, self-aware and brimming with positivity as she gears up to meet her daughter.

'I'm one of those people who gets anxiety about *everything* going on with my body. I'm not quite a hypochondriac but I'm definitely googling every symptom. I've got three co-workers who all just had their first kids in the last couple of years, so I bombard them with questions but, of course, everyone's pregnancy journey is different. I'm kind of left wondering, "Is this normal, or do I need to call the hospital?" It's been very helpful to find a bunch of other neurodivergent moms online, who also have anxiety. People who get it without making me feel like I should run to the doctor for every little thing – or worse, ignore something that actually matters.'

Jordan grew up around people with particular health and developmental needs. She was raised by her grandma and mum in California with her older brother and five boy cousins. Her brother has Kabuki syndrome, a rare genetic disorder that can result in slow physical growth and learning difficulties. One of her cousins has Down syndrome. Both her parents are neurodivergent. Jordan says she's not daunted by the possibility that her child might have health issues, but sometimes her anxiety and emotions can feel like a lot to handle.

'My first trimester was just horrible. Did I get more emotional? Yes. Was it what I expected? Nope. I didn't cry much – it was more like pure rage. I would get angry *so* fast that I had to hit pause on myself to avoid quitting my job or wrecking my relationship.

'Despite my anxiety, my pregnancy has been pretty straightforward and I feel as prepared as you can be for this experience. I'm not hypersensitive any more – I'm the opposite. I'm here to make this pregnancy as positive as possible for me, our daughter, all of us.'

We love hearing Jordan say that she's reached a place of calm about her health and wellbeing. There's no law that says every pregnant woman must blossom, or that having a peaceful pregnancy has to look a certain way. By the same token, being pregnant is not necessarily going to make health issues worse. For Jordan, getting to five months pregnant and feeling confident and well regulated feels like a gift. She's focused on enjoying a positive pregnancy, whatever comes.

Whether we feel healthy and happy in pregnancy will, of course, depend on a million factors, from our living situation, relationships and finances to our health pre-pregnancy. Access to good healthcare is a prerequisite but maternity services are overstretched in many countries. Being able to trust your healthcare professional can mean the difference between a straightforward and a stressful experience, but too many women in our community report feeling let down, dismissed and bullied. Being pregnant is a vulnerable stage in a woman's life, emotionally and physically, and yet women's health and wellbeing is still not prioritized or given enough resources.

If you're navigating an unfamiliar health system, there's an extra level of uncertainty. That was the case for Nicole Arruda, who is Brazilian but lives in London with her Brazilian husband and their two sons, aged four and two. 'I had a lot of questions and needed a lot of reassurance at the beginning of my pregnancy. It seemed strange to me that in the UK you don't see a doctor until the first scan at twelve weeks. I really relied on British friends to reassure me that that was normal in the National Health Service. Same thing towards the end. In Brazil you see doctors constantly in the last month, whether there are problems or not, so the more hands-off approach took a lot of getting used to.'

Whatever your circumstances, whether your pregnancy has been straightforward or tough, by the time you're approaching the end of your last trimester you'll be nursing a range of niggles both physical and emotional, and perhaps some worries about how everything is going. The changes to your body might be affecting your sleep, movement and mood. Your thoughts might be turning to looming events – giving birth and then actually meeting your baby. Maybe you want to ask your doctor or midwife about a new sensation you're feeling or a pain you're noticing. Or perhaps, like Jordan, you're reaching out to other women at the same stage in similar circumstances, or scrolling in search of info and comfort on social media.

For some women, the waiting game as they near their due date gives rise to excitement, maybe curiosity, a flutter of nerves. At the other end of the spectrum are women coping with significant anxiety. How people respond varies hugely, of course. As we saw in the last chapter, for some it helps to plan, for others it helps to trust that they will cope with events as they unfold. For many women, the big abstract questions about becoming a mother get boiled down into questions around their health and the health of their baby. Women want to know whether everything is going okay for them. It's a visceral response to the deep uncertainty they're facing – in other words, it makes perfect sense.

Talking to doctors, midwives and other professionals

Jordan said she didn't want to bother her doctor over every little thing, which is understandable. Nobody wants to spend their pregnancy in a waiting room unless they really have to, after all. On the other hand, Peanut Professional Kellie Leonard, who's based near Birmingham, UK, points out that many of us feel deeply isolated during pregnancy, which can fuel anxiety and eat into our wellbeing. Kellie, who is a biomedical scientist and writer on women's health, is also five months pregnant, so she has personal as well as professional experience to draw on. 'Midwifery services are often really stretched,' she says.

As well as overstretched services, too often there is still a mindset that doctors are authority figures and the system knows best. Women will put up with a lot rather than ask questions that risk us being painted as difficult. Peanut Professional Gail Janicola, who is a childbirth educator, and US national board-certified health and wellness coach, and has been working as a doula in Long Island, New York, for nearly 30 years, says, 'We've been led to believe that if someone went to medical school, we shouldn't question them. I understand that mindset – I used to be that person. But I now think it's crucial to see the value in being informed and empowered.'

Kellie discovered for herself how easy it is to end up feeling vulnerable when she developed hyperemesis gravidarum (extreme nausea and vomiting) at six weeks. 'I waited before I contacted my doctor,' Kellie told us, 'because I knew that sickness comes with the territory to a certain degree. But by week eight I couldn't take it any more. I couldn't get out of bed. I was put on cyclizine, which didn't work, and then I requested a different drug, which has helped a bit. I'm still struggling at 19 weeks though, and I really had to vouch for myself to get the more effective treatment.'

Seeking out reliable information is key and there are a lot of good resources online that you can consult before you see a doctor or other healthcare professional. It's important to bypass lifestyle influencers and instead go to qualified individuals or credible organizations you can trust, such as the websites of the UK's National Health Service; Canada, New Zealand and Australia's Medicare; or your healthcare provider in the US. If you're worried that you might end up down a rabbit hole or doomscrolling scary symptoms, enlist the help of a friend or a loved one. You could agree that you'll spend no more than 30 minutes searching for specific information together, and then draw a line. You might want to ask that person to come with you, if and when you do see a doctor. It's comforting to have company and if you forget to ask something, they can jump in. Black, Asian, Latina and Indigenous women are more likely to experience pregnancy and birth complications than white women, due to structural racism and bias. If this is you, you may find it particularly necessary to prepare yourself to keep asking questions and requesting more information and better solutions.

Kellie is clear that every pregnant woman, whatever her identity, wherever she is in the world, has a right to advocate for herself – in fact, we *must*, even if it's uncomfortable at first. 'Don't ever feel like you're bothering your medical support team,' she says. 'If you're worried or you're feeling horrible, you have every right to be heard.' Ninety-nine times out of a hundred, your fears can be put to bed and you'll be able to get back to enjoying pregnancy.

Being pregnant during tough times

Sometimes our worries are magnified by other issues. Life doesn't stop just because we're expecting a baby. If we're dealing with financial difficulties, insecure housing or emotional pressure from other big life events, we can end up in a spiral of worrying about worrying. Nobody wants their stress levels to affect their unborn child, but it's not always an option to keep calm and carry on.

Kerry Tay, who's from the UK but lives in Denver, Colorado, with her American husband and their 20-month-old son, Zander, found herself in exactly this situation. Kerry's relationship was long-distance for years, but in December 2019 she and her husband started making plans for her to move to the States. She arrived by the skin of her teeth in March 2020, just before Covid closed down international travel, having left in such a rush that she didn't have time to say goodbye properly to her family and friends. The couple moved in with Kerry's in-laws to wait out the pandemic; just over a year later, they were able to move into their own home. Not long afterwards, Kerry fell pregnant.

'Life was ridiculously intense, from arriving in the US, all the way through my pregnancy and into the first year of our son's life. My dad was diagnosed with terminal stage-four cancer during my second trimester. He was very, very sick and I desperately wanted to visit but I was advised by my doctors not to fly home to see him. He passed away six weeks before my son was born and I had to watch his funeral on a live stream. I didn't want stress to cause any complications, so I suppressed my feelings, but I think that made it harder in the long run. They blew up after Zander was born and the anxiety postpartum was overwhelming. My husband had his family here, but I had nobody. I felt so lonely watching everybody else bond. I just wish I'd allowed myself to feel a little more at the time and not worry so much about worrying, because it made everything harder.'

Kerry was bereaved and far from home. No wonder she found it hard to cope. But no pregnancy takes place in a bubble and there will always be stresses and strains. Prenatal anxiety and depression isn't talked about as much as the postnatal varieties, but if you're experiencing prolonged or recurring distress about any issue, please don't bottle it up. Speak to loved ones and seek out support, for your sake as much as your baby's.

Social media and online community – find the people who are right for you

Whether we're struggling to make ourselves heard by our medical team, dealing with extra emotional factors such as being bereaved or simply processing our questions and concerns, most of us will find ourselves late-night googling at some point during our pregnancy, in search of answers. There are fantastic communities and a lot of great content for women online. (We would say that, wouldn't we?!) But it's really important to seek out reliable and trustworthy information, and steer away from sensationalist, judgemental or extreme stories and opinions.

Gail notices that some of the women she works with end up feeling bombarded with contradictory information when they're relying on social media. 'One day they might feel confident based on something they've seen scrolling through TikTok or Instagram, but the next day, they see something different and start questioning everything.' To cut down on the risk of confusion and overwhelm, once you've found a good source of information and a few accounts you like and trust, it's worth sticking with them rather than seeking out more and more.

But as Kellie says, women are always going to look for the information and reassurance they need, and they'll find it wherever they can. When you're feeling alone and worried, there's nothing more comforting than going online to a trusted space, asking other people, 'Is this normal?' and receiving a flood of assurance that it totally is. Just make sure you choose your village carefully – online as you would anywhere else.

Don't surround yourself with people who are going to have a pity party or tell you to be a 'good patient'. Look for people who have critical thinking skills, have gained their knowledge from evidence-based information, and are open-minded. Look for those who will always see you as an individual.
— Gail Janicola, doula, childbirth educator

One tiny word of caution

We're sometimes told that pregnancy is not a medical condition, which is absolutely true as far as it goes, and many women sail through their whole pregnancy feeling well and happy, and that's wonderful. But as Kellie says, 'being pregnant is not a medical condition *until it is*'. For some women, those niggles and worries do develop into significant issues such as gestational diabetes (high blood sugar) or pre-eclampsia, which is a serious disorder related to high blood pressure that can begin during the second half of pregnancy or up to six weeks after birth. Gestational diabetes typically doesn't have strong symptoms, but if you are at risk you will be tested for it somewhere around 24–28 weeks. It's worth making sure you know the symptoms of pre-eclampsia (seeing spots, swelling in your hands or face, stomach pain and headaches), and report any worries to your doctor.

Every woman deserves to find the information and reassurance she needs, in a timely and reliable way. In public-health systems all over the world, that can prove difficult because of high demand and overstretched services. Where women do have access to private medical care, the resources may be easier to come by but there's no guarantee a doctor, midwife or nurse will be open-minded and willing to listen. Whatever your healthcare situation, you have the right to be heard and have your concerns and symptoms taken seriously and addressed. Here's Kellie again: 'You don't need to struggle on with any symptom just because you're pregnant or postpartum. Trust yourself, keep calm and be persistent.' Words to take to heart, wherever you live.

In a nutshell . . .

Asking 'Is this normal?' is totally normal. Whatever the issue, whatever the worry, you're not the only one. We can guarantee that there are thousands of other women with exactly the same questions and worries.

Look for trustworthy information. Think about how you can fulfil your needs for reliable information and reassurance. Be picky about who you welcome into your village and always go for expertise over noise.

If any symptom is getting on top of you, don't feel you have to put up with it. That includes anxiety or stress. You deserve to be heard. Speak to a doctor or a counsellor and let them help you deal with any issues.

Be your own advocate, or ask a loved one to advocate for you. Pregnancy can make you feel vulnerable and it does carry risks. We all need to advocate for ourselves, but that counts double for women from marginalized groups. Is there anyone who can be your ally in tricky situations or conversations?

CHAPTER 4

Planning the unplannable

On childbirth, nerves and realistic expectations

Preparing to give birth is probably the ultimate challenge for those of us who are navigating the excitement and anxiety of late pregnancy. At Peanut we're not in the business of horror stories about childbirth or relentlessly downbeat depictions of motherhood. We just believe in the value and necessity of honesty because we know that's what matters to our community. And the honest truth is that childbirth still carries some risks for mother and baby. Its realities are still shrouded in secrecy, despite more opportunities for women to discuss their experiences. For some of us, giving birth can be empowering and euphoric; for others, it's gruelling. For everyone, it's a physical and emotional endurance test. But at the end we get to meet the most important person in our lives: our baby.

In every culture across time and all over the world, giving birth has been recognized as a profound transition. It will remake every woman who goes through it. No wonder we approach the subject with a mixture of apprehension and excitement. What could be more personal, or more crucial, or more potentially overwhelming and scary? Where do you begin? Is it even worth *trying* to prepare for something so intrinsically unpredictable when you've probably heard plenty of stories about birth plans that dissolved on impact with reality? Short answer – yes, it is, as we'll see.

Morgan, who we met in the first chapter, had her second child just six weeks ago. Her older daughter is now coming up for two and a half but Morgan's memories of her birth are still vivid, and she's very clear about how and why she approached things differently second time around.

'I wasn't frightened when I ended up having a C-section with my first daughter, but I did feel vulnerable and ill-equipped. I had focused all my planning on the scenario I wanted, and I hadn't looked at the one I didn't. I'd researched how to have a non-intervention, pain relief-free birth and I ended up being induced, with an epidural and an emergency C-section. The really scary bit was that my daughter had to spend three days in the NICU, which isn't long compared to what some babies and their families endure, but still, it was tough. When things went sideways, I felt even more shocked and frightened for not having allowed my mind to go there.

'Second time around, I had a doula who helped me plan for a VBAC [vaginal birth after caesarean] *and* a scheduled C-section because my doctor, who I love, laid out some ground rules. If I didn't go into spontaneous labour by the middle of week 39, I was having a C-section. I felt fine with that. I had the mindset of knowing that I couldn't control my birth story but at least I'd really thought it through. When the scheduled day arrived and there was no sign of me going into labour, I was like, "Let's get on with this." My daughter screamed as they were getting her out, and I just started crying because my older daughter never made a sound as she was being born. And that was my main worry. When my doctor and my doula had asked me what I hoped for this time, I said, "Not to have to go to the NICU."'

No amount of planning would stop us panicking if our newborn was being taken to neonatal intensive care. While scare stories are unhelpful and not representative of how most women experience childbirth, allowing ourselves to think through different situations rather than focusing only on the best-case scenario can leave us less exposed to anxiety, as Morgan discovered.

We're not here to tell you what you already know: that there are antenatal classes and you can speak to your midwife or hire a doula. We're certainly not here to scare you, guilt you or judge you for your choices (epidural, no epidural – it's nobody's business but yours); only to introduce you to women who have approached this most intensely personal question in any number of different ways. And show you that, as ever, you're not alone. We'll also be hearing more of the expert voice of Gail Janicola, doula, childbirth educator, coach and mother of three grown-up children, who acts as a mentor for women readying to give birth.

So whether you're excited, nervous, dreading it, in denial or all of the above, take a deep breath and settle down to think about how you would like to prepare for childbirth.

Nerves are normal, but so are positive experiences

'I watched my siblings being born, first when I was 11 and then again when I was 14 and 17. I saw it all go down in real time, which is both slightly horrifying and educational for a pre-teen,' says Jordan Shane, who we met in a previous chapter. 'My mom's first birth after me should've been a C-section. At one point there were 17 doctors waiting outside the room.

But her next was very straightforward, so I've seen the good and the not so good and I know that my mom and my siblings are just fine.'

As Jordan says, seeing your mum give birth when you're just 11 yourself is definitely going to teach you a thing or two, but it's an unusual way to get informed. What most of us know about childbirth comes from bland or ideologically driven antenatal classes on the one hand and TV dramas and online forums on the other, where lurid plotlines and negative experiences have the highest currency. Unless we're medical professionals ourselves, we probably won't have been around birthing people until the day we give birth ourselves. No wonder we're nervous. That lack of honest information means that some of us are heading towards childbirth feeling unnecessarily frightened, while others are wishing for a fantasy birth that may not happen. We all deserve better.

Women's concerns are often made worse by the fact that, as we saw in the previous chapter, many of us feel we're not being heard by our medical providers and are simply being pushed through the system. Planning our child's birth allows us to be an active participant in a process that too often feels impersonal and focused on the bare minimum outcomes – a healthy baby and a healthy mum. Every woman wants this for her baby and herself, but we also want to have some say over the quality of the experience. Perhaps we'd like to aim for peaceful, empowering – even revelatory. It's perfectly possible to have these and many other kinds of positive experiences giving birth; it's just that there are no guarantees. That doesn't mean it's silly to aspire to them, simply that it's also sensible to consider different treatment options and think through various outcomes.

Stephani Evans, who now lives with her family in rural

Montana in the US, has had two very positive experiences. She gave birth to her first daughter in a birthing centre two hours' drive from their home when the family were living in Yosemite National Park. It was the closest facility that could provide the experience she hoped for. 'I wanted to have a birth without interventions, taking as much time as I needed. My midwife and doula, who were both registered nurses, were really experienced. They did their checks, but they mostly left me to get on with it until the time when my daughter was about to come out and then they helped me deliver her in the water tub. My husband caught her, at which point we realized that she'd been sunny-side-up all along.

'The second time, I had a home birth with a different but equally great team of two midwives, one of whom was in training and was also a registered nurse and doula. We had a birth tub set up, but my daughter just came so fast and furious that the tub was not relaxing. I knelt down on the floor with one leg up, Captain Morgan style, and once again my husband caught her as she came out. Our older daughter was with us during some early stages. She was giving me snuggles, which was such a loving and nurturing experience. She did choose to go and sit in her room at one point when I hit transition and I was shouting a bit, and that felt like the right thing to happen. We also hired a birth photographer. I find it so moving to look at those photos now. I feel amazed at what I did. At what we all did. It was an incredible experience to have as a family, and I feel so lucky to have had two positive experiences because not everyone does. I knew at the time that I might not. I mean, I obviously made certain choices and hoped and planned for things to be a certain way, but I tried to keep a flexible mindset. I wouldn't change a thing, but as I say, I feel lucky. We can't always control how things go.'

Stephani's right that there's always a certain amount of luck involved in how any of our birthing experiences develop, but as she, Jordan, Morgan and Gail agree, as long as you have the right people in your team and you keep an open mind, you will have done everything possible to ensure that you have a good experience – whatever happens.

The Sticky Stuff:
Vaginal birth versus C-section

If you're currently planning your birthing experience, your first and most fundamental decision is whether to aim for a vaginal delivery or opt for a C-section. You've almost certainly got a strong preference one way or the other. While it should really be nobody's business but your own, based purely on the advice of your doctor and your own preferences, it's one of those questions that arouses strong feelings and opinions. That can make it into a flashpoint for emotions and even conflict, whether that's with your loved ones, other mums, or within yourself.

First of all, while many women in our community hope to have a vaginal birth, and in countries like the US, Canada, Australia and the UK, vaginal births are more common, the rate of C-sections is going up all over the world. In the UK, for example, C-sections increased to 37.8 per cent of births in 2023, up from 34.7 the previous year. In the US that percentage was 32.4, up from 32.1 in 2022.

Then there's the difference between a C-section you schedule and one that your medical team decide is a necessity because your baby just needs to get born, *now*. Both elective and emergency C-sections are going up in the UK. In 2023, 16 per cent of UK births were elective caesareans and 19 per cent were emergency C-sections.

To put it plainly, one in five women in the UK ended up having an emergency C-section. Rates are similar in Australia, Canada and the US. So while there's an element of decision-making here, it's also true that we might end up giving birth via a C-section when we hadn't wanted or planned to. And given those stats, it's crucial to be prepared and to try to accept that while we have preferences, we might not always be able to make the choice we prefer. The question then becomes not which is better or even which do I want, but how can I ensure I'm ready for either?

Morgan found herself in this situation, and her wisdom is worth going back to. 'I'm now part of a support group for pregnant and postpartum moms,' she told us. 'There are four ladies who will be giving birth in the next couple of months. We were discussing our hopes and plans the other day when the subject of C-sections came up. One of my friends said to another, "But you're not planning a C-section, right, so this doesn't apply to you." "Neither was I," I reminded them.'

Ideas about what's 'normal' and 'best' in terms of childbirth can and do change over time and are different in different areas of the world. In many South American countries like Argentina and Brazil, for example, elective C-sections are now the norm. Jordan told us about chatting with her mum about C-sections. Jordan's mum had strong opinions about what Jordan should aim for. She stressed the benefits of a vaginal delivery without pain relief, on the grounds that it was easier to bond with your baby that way. She had given birth to her babies in California at a time when this was the message from health professionals and she, like all of us, just wanted to do the right thing by her babies. But as Jordan also said, her mother's next delivery after her was highly complex and really should have been a C-section. Perhaps knowing all this has made it easier for Jordan to be relaxed about her birth plan and set aside an attachment to one particular way of birthing.

We know that far too many women see not being able to deliver their child vaginally as a failure. If this is you, or you worry it might be, we hope that Peanut Professional Dr Lisa Folden's words will land with you. She's a physical therapist and body image coach who works with mums from her base in North Carolina, US. And she has very clear thoughts on the shame that mothers carry because of beliefs about their body, its appearance and capacities. 'If your body isn't doing what you want it to, you might feel you are a failure. That is not a fair or realistic belief to hold about yourself or the world. I want people to understand that we don't have the control we think we have over our bodies. That goes for everything from being able to sustain weight loss long-term to having a vaginal delivery. Many of the factors that lead to those outcomes are not under our control.'

We know that women thrive when they're informed and empowered to play an active part in planning for birth. We also know that having an open mind and a non-judgemental attitude to their own body and outcomes can mean the difference between feeling good and feeling not so good about their birthing experience. Whether you're planning or recovering, we wish you a gentle conversation with yourself and others. Be kind to yourself and to the other mums out there. However you give birth, you're amazing.

Who gets to be in your birth team?

For Gail, a birth team includes everyone with whom you discuss your plans, those you invite to support you through the process (both personally and professionally) and then surround yourself with in the immediate postpartum period (again, friends, family and anybody you choose to hire). It's a broad definition and might be many people but remember, you're not obliged to share your hopes and plans widely, or listen to everyone's opinions. Your doctor's opinion matters. Your partner, if you have one, is definitely worth a listen. Beyond that, you're the one who gets to call the shots and set the tone. What will feel best for you? Giving birth at home, or in a clinic or hospital? Who would you like to be there? Your mother, your sister? (Hint: only people who are completely supportive of you and all your decisions, as well as being a calming presence during labour, should make the shortlist.)

Gail advises being very selective about who you talk to. If your mother is not on board with your preference for a vaginal delivery after a C-section, for example, and is telling you that it's dangerous and she has no idea why you're even considering it, maybe she's not going to be part of your team. 'You don't have to disassociate from your mother, but you don't have to include her in your village either. You can pick and choose who gets to be in your team. It's important for women to feel empowered to have these conversations.'

That said, not every decision is under your control. If you are giving birth in a public hospital, you won't be able to guarantee that the midwife who attends your birth will be the same person you've been talking to during your pregnancy, for example. If you can afford it, a doula can be an invaluable source of support. Trainee doulas will sometimes take on a job for a reduced rate as part of their qualification process, so don't assume you can't afford it without checking.

My mom, dad, sister and doula accompanied me in the labor room. I was worried that my dad being there would make things awkward but when the time came I didn't care because I was in pain, and I was focused. Labor was tough but giving birth was such a beautiful experience. As my daughter was delivered, my family and I all started crying. I knew then that she was truly loved and motherhood was going to be good.

— Jasmin J., US

67

To birth plan or not to birth plan?

We all know that not everything in life goes according to plan – and that truism counts double for childbirth. Plenty of women in our community roll their eyes when you say the words 'birth plan'. As Michelle, our founder, put it, 'Nothing about my first birth went according to plan, so I did feel a bit sceptical about the worth of my birth plan immediately afterwards.' But as she also recognizes, just because the plan didn't describe the experience she ended up having, that didn't mean it was a waste of time. Gail uses the analogy of preparing for a vacation. 'A flight might get cancelled or it might rain the entire time you're at the beach, so you have to be prepared to pivot. But you certainly wouldn't surrender your ideal vision and forgo the planning entirely, just because an unforeseen circumstance was a possibility. And planning could, in some cases, decrease the odds of a preventable issue. That's how I feel about birth plans. They have far-reaching benefits. At the very least, they open up a dialogue between you and your team. They're not rigid; they're more like a list of considerations.'

Morgan agrees. 'I would suggest that it's worth hiring a doula to help you with a birth plan, even if you can't afford for them to attend the birth as well. It is so valuable to sit down with an expert who can help you think through lots of different scenarios and answer your questions, maybe ask you about things that you've never even thought of.'

Gail cautions that rather than thinking of a birth plan as something you put together the month before your due date, 'birth planning should be an ongoing process that starts early in pregnancy, where you gather information, communicate with your loved ones and caregivers and build confidence.

The plan will likely change as you learn more, just as you might adjust your vacation plans as you discover new places to go. While things often don't go as planned during birth, *having* a plan allows you to make on-the-spot decisions more easily and change course if the need arises. You'll be informed, able to have meaningful conversations with your caregivers and loved ones, and feel less fearful and more in control.'

If you have time and energy, it's also worth thinking about who will be there for you after the birth. Researching lactation consultants, postpartum doulas or therapists who specialize in postpartum anxiety will take the pressure off later if you do need professional help. You could also ask friends and family for specific and time-bound help in the first few weeks. Having these conversations ahead of time, when your emotions are not so fraught, helps to dial down the stress.

And if all this talk of planning is making you feel even more tired, we're here to tell you that rest, relaxation and self-care should now officially be your top priorities. Get as much sleep as you can, keep doing gentle exercise if possible, maybe download a meditation app or simply spend time outside in nature. Whatever is going to help you feel calm, centred and rested. Childbirth is hard work, physically and emotionally. Allow yourself to be as well as you can be, for your own sake primarily, but also your family's. Mums can't look after everyone else if they don't look after themselves first. It's not selfish — it's necessary, especially during pregnancy and postpartum.

We hope that the stories in this chapter reassure you that there are many ways to have a good birthing experience. In one sense every woman births her baby alone, which is partly why it feels so daunting, but on the other hand, as Morgan and Stephani emphasize, it's a team effort. The village really comes into its own when it comes to giving birth. Above all, you're more resilient and more powerful than you know. You've got this.

In a nutshell . . .

Feeling nervous is totally normal, being informed will help.
Make a minute-by-minute birth plan if that's what helps you.
Just remember the value of planning for a range of scenarios. If you're not a planner, that's fine too, but informing yourself about the potential outcomes and your choices can help you feel empowered and prepared when the time comes.

Steer away from horror stories and any approach you find unconvincing. If you're not getting the information you need in an antenatal group, ask questions. If you're still uncomfortable, look for a different group.

Giving birth is easier with the right people around you.
Assemble your team carefully and think in terms of who you're talking to in the run-up and who's going to be there afterwards, as well as the people who will be with you on the day. Prioritize yourself. This is no time to be a people-pleaser.

Looking after yourself is essential. If you haven't yet started a self-care routine, now is the time to do it. Many of us find it hard to take time for ourselves without feeling guilty, especially when it comes to rest, eating well and relaxing. Use this time to practise facing down any guilt you might have over self-care, because looking after your own needs is going to be crucial over the next couple of years.

PART TWO
The first few weeks

CHAPTER 5

What just happened?

On being in a state of shock

The transition from being pregnant to no longer being pregnant is one of the most extreme and rapid transformations that any human being can go through and yet it still gets played down in our culture. We all know it's a big deal, of course, but too often its complexity gets reduced to 'So long as there's a healthy baby and a healthy mother, everything else is irrelevant.' But that's a bare minimum of what we deserve and a totally inadequate description of what happens and why it matters. The reality of giving birth and the first few days afterwards is messy, bewildering, ecstatic and overwhelming. It's life at its most raw and extreme. No wonder so many of us end up reeling, swinging between emotional highs and lows. We're basically in a state of shock.

That was exactly how Becca Ajidahun experienced the first days of her daughter's life. Becca is 34 and lives with her husband and their nearly two-year-old in east London. She's a cheerful and pragmatic person but her voice still changes when she talks about the overwhelm of the first few days after giving birth.

'It was the third day after Sienna was born when everything hit me at once. My milk came in, my emotions surged and it felt as if a wave of hormones was crashing over me. We had just found out that Sienna had a heart murmur and the doctors wanted to check it again, so I was frightened about that. I was struggling to keep it together but we had family coming over – my partner's family, who I was still getting comfortable with. When they walked in, I was holding the baby, trying to smile. As soon as I saw them, I burst into tears. One of my husband's relatives asked, "Why are you crying?" In hindsight I'm sure they were just concerned, but at the time I thought to myself, *What do you mean, why am I crying? Do you not realize what I've just been through, and what we're all going through right now?*

'I ended up retreating to the bedroom. I let my husband take over – he entertained the family, passed the baby around and brought her to me from time to time, so he could check up on how I was. Which wasn't great. I sat there feeling sore from the birth, with my boobs swollen, unable to stop crying. I had never experienced anything like it. My emotions were totally out of control. I think I was in shock, from giving birth, from fear that there might be something seriously wrong with Sienna, all the hormonal and physical changes. Everything was overwhelming.

'My husband asked his family to leave once they'd had a cuddle and a cup of tea. He didn't try to force me to come out, or socialize. He just said, do what you need to do. He understood completely. And things did get better, fortunately. Sienna is fine now. But I still remember the utter vulnerability of that day. It was awful.'

Your first days of motherhood are likely to contain extremes of vulnerability you may never have encountered before. There is a rawness to this time that sticks in the mind even years later. It might be a hazy memory, more like a feeling than a clear recollection, of peaks of joy and amazement contrasted with troughs of shock and overwhelm. For those mothers who birthed their children, there is the physicality of childbirth and the storm of hormones that swirls afterwards; for every mother there is the emotional earthquake of meeting your child and grasping the fact that they are now here, in the world, and they are *your responsibility*. That's what Becca was talking about when she recalled sitting alone in her bedroom, her body bruised and tender, overcome by the impossibility of having to pretend that life was normal and everything was the same. No wonder she couldn't stop crying.

So many women tell us that they're unprepared for the shock of being just postpartum. Not just the pain or the exhaustion or the disbelief about the experience that, if you've laboured to give birth to your child, you've just endured, but the almost psychedelic *weirdness* of it. The jolt to reality that comes along with having had another person inside you who is now outside, staring back at you with a look so intense it makes you think of an ancient soul in a tiny new body.

So, if you've just worked through labour, congratulations to you! You are a total hero right now. Perhaps you're full of amazement at what your body has managed to do, maybe even feeling like 'a triumphant goddess', in the words of one mum who couldn't believe how much better her second birthing experience was than her first. Or you might be feeling that your body let you down. Maybe you're disappointed that things didn't go the way you'd hoped they would. Whatever you're feeling, you made it. You and your baby are on the other side of that elemental experience we call childbirth.

You may well be sitting with a strong sense of surprise that giving birth, like pregnancy, has not turned out to be quite as it's depicted in films or even as it's presented in antenatal classes or hypnobirthing courses. It can take so much longer. It can be so much more painful, but in rich and complex and interesting ways. It can be deeply frightening, because even in societies with advanced medical practices, it is still risky; but also so much more empowering. Giving birth is just so much *more* than we ever get told. It's as if we don't have the language to describe it, or more likely, we aren't in the habit of facing up to its complex reality.

> *You're bleeding and your boobs hurt and you're sweating and then suddenly you're cold because your hormones are doing crazy things and you're like, I smell bad, but I know I showered. Didn't I?*
>
> **— Kylie H., US**

'Why did nobody tell me . . .?'

As you enter days two, three and four after giving birth you'll probably be coming up against a series of *Why did nobody tell me?* moments. *Why did nobody tell me that breastfeeding can be agonizing until you get used to it? Why did nobody tell me that there would be a hormonal crash three days afterwards that sends my mood plummeting and makes me feel like I'm going completely insane? And what's with the haemorrhoids?* There are lots of these moments, and while not every woman will experience them all, they're common enough to make us wonder why they don't get discussed in the books and classes for pregnant women. 'What was the point of ante-natal classes if they're not going to tell you these things?' as Kat from Manchester in the UK put it. (We're with you, Kat.)

The answer, we suspect, is that often, all the focus is on the baby rather than the baby *and* the mother. 'I was quite shocked by how there wasn't much interest in how I was doing, or information about what I should expect afterwards,' said Kat. 'I had no idea that there would be so many physical symptoms *after* giving birth. Contractions, for example. Three days after my second child was born, I started feeling strong contractions. I didn't know what was going on but luckily I had a couple of mum friends I could ask. One of them told me she'd felt the same thing. She'd asked her health visitor, who told her that it was caused by the womb returning to its usual size. That was a real *Why did nobody tell me?* moment.' Kat shook her head in slight disbelief. 'Or night sweats. I didn't know that's also very common. Your hormones are all over the place, and that can trigger excessive sweating. I had to change my bedsheets every day for a week. It would have been nice to know.'

'We still don't have the honest conversations about birth and postpartum that would actually be helpful for women,' says Kellie Leonard, the biomedical scientist and writer on women's health we met previously. 'It's getting better, especially where women are able to freely exchange their stories, but in a lot of media, women's experiences of childbirth and recovery are either underplayed as something to bounce back from as quickly as possible, or presented as a horror story. It's as if these are the only two options available, but neither is necessarily representative of the majority of experiences. They either scare people or enforce unrealistic expectations of birth and postpartum. I think it's helpful and empowering to talk about a broader range of experiences with a lot more honesty. That means we can all feel less worried and less alone.'

Kat agrees. 'My second birth wasn't terrible, at least in terms of outcomes, but it wasn't great. It was almost like

I was a problem rather than a person. I asked for an epidural but when I was given it, my blood pressure and heart rate both began to drop. I could see that the staff were worried. They told me they'd never seen anyone react like that and they would have to withdraw the epidural immediately. Which is not what you want to hear when you're in labour. For a moment I was really scared. I remember thinking, *I can't die, I've got my son at home and he needs me.* Fortunately the doctors were able to stabilize the situation but it was frightening and I wasn't given any reassurance. Perhaps it wasn't a big deal for the professionals, but it was for me. When I asked if there was any alternative pain relief, the midwife made me feel I was being demanding and I should just get on with it. I did eventually get something, but it wasn't effective and it made me feel really strange, as if I wasn't there at all. The whole thing was kind of traumatic. I felt very scared, almost bullied, and I was in much more pain than I'd prepared for. To be honest, I think it was the way I was treated that was the most difficult thing.'

Kat saw a health visitor at home, about ten days after giving birth. They did ask about her birth experience, but the only comment was that she could complain to the hospital if she wished. Kat was deep into caring for her two children under two. She didn't want to think about what had happened, especially since, as she said, 'Everything was fine. I mean, it had been tough and I had a lot of stitches – Flo was a big baby – but I was home and I was feeling a little better every day.' Kat hasn't made a complaint and has never talked about any of it again with a professional. 'I don't know how I feel about it, really,' she says. 'It was almost as if nobody had time to even listen to me.'

Kellie points to the way that women become invisible after

giving birth. 'The scrutiny when you're pregnant can be very intrusive, but it can also feel like you're being cared for. Once you give birth, all the focus from healthcare professionals and family and friends shifts to the baby. It almost doesn't matter about the mother's recovery; if she's had a C-section and she's bleeding or she tore during delivery and her stitches are now infected. Babies are important, don't get me wrong,' says Kellie, smiling, 'and their health and wellbeing need to be monitored, but the same goes for new mums.'

So it helps to know what you might be dealing with. The postpartum recovery period is officially classified as the first six weeks after giving birth, at the end of which you'll have a check-up with your doctor. In reality, recovery can take way longer. Your experience will depend on loads of variables, including how you gave birth. If you had a vaginal delivery, you may be over the worst of the soreness within three weeks, but if you tore or had an episiotomy, when the doctor makes a small cut in your perineum, then you will have stitches, and those stitches need to be kept clean in order to prevent infections. Not an easy thing to do, especially when you're likely to be bleeding for at least two weeks after birth. If you had a C-section, then you've had major abdominal surgery and have a scar that needs careful aftercare. You shouldn't be doing any heavy lifting for six weeks afterwards, but as generations of women have discovered, that's almost impossible to avoid if you have an older child in need of cuddles. You're going to need stocks of maternity pads for bleeding, dressings for your scar, paracetamol for pain relief (as a minimum – ask your doctor what else is safe to take and available), post-surgical cleansing agent for stitches or scar, ice packs to sit on, cream for those haemorrhoids and your biggest, most comfy cotton knickers.

Recovering from childbirth takes time and patience, but of course time is in short supply when you have a newborn, and possibly older children as well. Energy and emotional bandwidth are also limited. You might not even have the capacity to *notice* your symptoms and feelings any more, let alone google them. As Kellie says, 'You don't want to ask yourself, *Oh, am I getting migraines, is that a problem, or do I maybe have depression?* You just want to get on with looking after your baby. But *you* need looking after too. Whether you have tricky symptoms or not, whether you feel fine but just a bit tired or really horrible, you've had a big experience and you deserve to look after yourself as well as your baby.'

> *The body is CRAZY. Experiencing postpartum has been a huge eye-opener for me. I never thought it would be this difficult. I thought the pregnancy was going to be the hard part. That was a breeze.*
>
> **— Samantha W., US**

Accept any offers of care – and show *yourself* the love

'I didn't lift a finger for a month after I gave birth. I felt like a queen.' That's Anessa, who we met previously. She lives in Montreal among a community of mostly West African immigrants, where traditional practices of caring for pregnant and postpartum mums are still very much the norm. Postpartum doulas have become more popular over the last few years. Their role is inspired by this traditional practice of honouring the new mother with care and support. They're not medically trained and their primary role is not to look after the baby, more to provide a listening ear and help with practical tasks. Doulas might stay overnight so a mother can get some uninterrupted sleep, discuss worries about the impact of a new baby on an older child, or batch-cook dinner for the next week.

We don't all have the financial resources to hire a doula or come from a culture where extended care is available, but it can benefit all of us to know what's considered 'normal' in different places. It can help to raise our expectations and empower us to ask for and accept help, if we know that such help is a regular part of life for some women. If a family member, friend or your partner offers to run you a bath and bring you a cup of tea after you've put the baby down, cut yourself some slack and say yes. You deserve it. Whether you became a mother three days ago, or three years ago, you absolutely still deserve it! You don't need anyone's permission to treat yourself tenderly, indulge yourself or follow your instincts for what will aid your recovery or soothe your body, mind and spirit.

It's not a sign of weakness, failure or not coping if you find yourself weeping uncontrollably as Becca did on day three. It's a sign that you've just been through a huge and challenging transition. Your day three (or four, five, six, etc.) will look similar but also different from anyone else's, and that's part of the great thing about modern motherhood. We can learn from and cheerlead for so many different women and their families, knowing that we have a lot in common alongside our differences. Whether you're facing day three after you gave birth yourself, day three since you thanked your surrogate for their part in birthing your child, or it's been three days since you did the final handover with the foster carers, we salute you. You're doing great.

Do not ignore your own welfare

We hope that the first few days as a new family are spent getting to know your baby or child, snuggling, cuddling and loving them as you bond. We hope you are looked after and appreciated for the incredible achievement of bringing yourself and your child to this point. We hope you're able to start to work through your feelings and begin to heal any and every part of you that needs to recover. This is an intense time and it's easy to be so focused on your child that your own physical, mental and emotional state gets pushed into the background. But please, without wanting to alarm you, remember that this is also a vulnerable time, especially if you have recently given birth. Don't ignore any increase in pain or distress. Talk to someone, and call your midwife, health visitor or doctor.

Three days after Stefani C. and her son were discharged from hospital, she began to experience chills, sweating, sleepiness and dizziness. 'I felt terrible but all I wanted was to take care of my baby, so I put it on the backburner for a day or so,' she said. Stefani, who we'll be hearing more from in a later chapter, lives in Northern California with her fiancé Sergio and their son Matteo, who is now eight months old.

'I wondered whether I had mastitis,' she continued, 'but about a week after Matteo was born, I woke up and I knew something was really wrong. My body felt like it was still asleep. My headache was so awful that I could barely walk. I told my partner and then my mom and she said, "You've got to get to hospital." So my fiancé drove me there. He practically had to carry me to the car.

'I had gotten a pelvic infection. They told me it was a

82

good thing I had gone in because I almost had sepsis. The worst moment for me was when they did a pelvic exam. I had a second-degree tear from the birth and they had told me, you know, don't put anything up there, and then the doctor did the pelvic exam, and she wasn't gentle about it. So I started bleeding even more. But they helped me, I got a bunch of fluids and a course of antibiotics. I was in hospital for a couple of days. I missed my son so much. I felt so bad about that. But thank goodness I listened to my mom, because sepsis . . .' Stefani's voice trailed off. 'It can be really bad.'

It sure can. Please, if you are feeling worse as the first week or two go by, don't hesitate. Your baby is a precious, valuable and important being. So are you.

In a nutshell . . .

Your whole world just changed – give yourself some grace. Whatever your route to motherhood, the shock of meeting your child and confronting your new reality can feel overwhelming. You're likely to be very tired and very emotional. Be gentle with yourself as you get to know your child and begin to adjust to your new life.

If you've given birth, take extra care of your physical and emotional needs. Childbirth is a huge experience, even when it goes smoothly. Don't underestimate the impact on your body and mind of the physical process and the hormonal changes. Stock up on postpartum medical essentials, rest as much as you can and don't be surprised if you feel high as a kite with happiness one minute and despairing the next.

If you've experienced some degree of trauma, whether that's a birth injury or poor treatment by medical staff, you're going to feel extra vulnerable. Talk to your family and friends, your health visitor and your doctor at your six-week check-up. Don't bottle up your feelings or tell yourself that they don't matter so long as you and your baby are 'fine'.

If you feel worse as the days go on, go to the hospital. There are small but significant risks in the postpartum period, to your physical and mental health. Don't ignore symptoms or put off seeing a doctor.

CHAPTER 6
Why do I feel so shit?

*On hormonal mood crashes, PND
and postpartum anxiety*

Grace Williams is a 23-year-old community staff nurse from Dorset in the UK, where she lives with her partner and their baby son. Grace wasn't expecting to get pregnant when she did and wasn't sure she was ready for motherhood, but she had a smooth pregnancy. Unfortunately, when she experienced a difficult birth her mental health took a terrible turn for the worse.

'The night after my son was born, I looked down at him and thought, "This can't have come out of me." It's horrible to say it, but I did not feel anything for him. I'd ended up having a C-section that I felt had been forced on me. The epidural went in too high up my spine, so I couldn't feel anything below my neck. I couldn't even move my arms to hug my baby when they put him on my chest. I tried again and again to feed him but he couldn't latch and it was so painful, so of course he was hungry. Neither of us got any sleep that night. My partner wasn't able to stay with us, and I felt so lonely. I looked at the baby and just thought, "How did this happen?" I'd gone from stroking my bump for six months to feeling absolutely nothing.

'I spent the first three weeks of my son's life with the recurring thought that everyone would be better off if I wasn't there any more. I knew I wasn't a risk to him, but I didn't believe I was a benefit to him either. I just felt completely disconnected. I told my health visitor, "This isn't what I was told it was going to be like." You're never fully prepared for becoming a mother, but everything that happened to us – the birthing experience, the infection I got afterwards, the persistent feeling that the doctors weren't listening – was making a bad situation a hundred times worse. I didn't want to die exactly, but I couldn't see the point of living.'

Grace's son is now 11 months old. He's thriving and so is she; the two of them are fully bonded. She tells her birth story with a mixture of dark humour and disbelief, still not quite understanding how a succession of chance events and some questionable clinical decisions led to her feeling like her family might be better off without her.

So what happened? Grace laboured at home for 24 hours before being transferred to hospital, where a doctor steered her away from a hormone drip and towards a C-section. She suspected that the needs of the doctor in training who was also present were being prioritized over hers. She felt she wasn't being listened to. The situation was made worse by her own unique circumstances. 'I was desperate not to give birth in hospital because I find them very triggering. I spent a lot of my childhood in oncology wards after my mum was diagnosed with cancer at the age of 36. She died when I was 16, and when I found out I was pregnant aged 21, I had some serious doubts. I absolutely did not feel grown-up enough to be a mother myself. My partner and I eventually decided that yes, we were going to be parents. I was flagged to the prenatal mental health services, but I sailed through pregnancy despite chronic sickness. Everything was great until I ended up in hospital.'

It is heartbreaking to hear how desperate Grace felt, but although her experience was extreme, mental health difficulties and emotional distress are common for new mothers. We hear people's stories in our community all the time. Some women know they're in crisis, others are asking, *Is it normal to feel this bad?* Women's symptoms and experiences vary hugely, from psychotic breaks and feelings of dissociation to feeling persistently down or anxious.

One thread that runs through all the stories is people's sense that they're letting their family and themselves down by feeling bad. And that's one strand of this scary experience for which we really can offer a simple answer: if this is you, or has been you – please know that you are not letting anyone down. Is it normal to feel low, miserable, disconnected, anxious or crazy after becoming a mother? Yes – it absolutely is. Do you have to put up with that, deny it or try to fix it alone? No – you absolutely do not. We only have one aim in this section of the book: to help you feel safe and seen, so that you can find the help you deserve. Please know that while postpartum anxiety and depression can feel all-consuming, you can and will recover. And if you've suffered before and are currently pregnant again and worried about a repeat, be reassured that you're not condemned to struggle just because you did last time.

Even if it's normal, it still feels awful

Some degree of emotional turmoil and low mood after childbirth is so common that it even has a cutesy name:

'the baby blues'. Sudden hormonal changes combined with the physical shock, tiredness and emotional overwhelm can produce weepiness and feeling down. This tends to happen within a few days of giving birth and clear up within a couple of weeks. If low mood or anxious thoughts get worse or persist beyond a month or so, it might be that you're heading towards postnatal depression or anxiety. This too is very common and, again, affects people on a sliding scale from mild to severe. It can feel scary and sap your joy with your baby, setting you up for more spirals of worry. That was where Becca Ajidahun found herself, six weeks after her daughter was born.

'I was having loads of intrusive thoughts. I kept imagining terrible scenarios that were going to happen to me and the baby. On one occasion we were on our way to meet my health visitor. I walked past a building site and I was like, what if a hammer falls and lands on my baby? Or what if there's a crazy man in that car and he knocks into us? I told my health visitor, who said that it was very common and I could self-refer to talking therapy, which I never did. I was just in survival mode, so I didn't get around to it. And by the time I could, things had calmed down a bit.'

Becca's experience was unsettling and unpleasant. 'It was scary to be thinking these things and scary not to be able to stop. I didn't feel like myself and I struggled to cope,' she says. Thankfully, within a few weeks Becca's mood was generally tracking upwards. In some sense what she experienced was *totally* normal, exactly the kind of thing that biologists suggest comes with the brain and hormonal territory of being a new mother. But just because it's normal doesn't mean it's easy to handle or unimportant, and simply knowing that it's common doesn't always help. As Becca said, a little bit more information, reassurance and kindness from her health visitor would have been great.

The fact is that while emotional distress is very common, every woman's experience is different, and the range of symptoms and their spectrum of severity is huge. It's hard to figure out whether we're dealing with a passing case of baby blues or something more serious if we're not given clear information and guidelines, but the reality is that there are no hard lines between these conditions, and calling the difference is highly personal. As always, yours is the opinion that matters most, but your doctor would definitely want to know about it if you're still feeling horrible three weeks after you've given birth. Kellie Leonard says, 'The crucial thing to know is that while mood swings, low energy, low mood and all the rest of it are very common, no mother needs to suffer in silence. There are effective and safe treatments for postpartum depression and anxiety that you can take while breastfeeding. If you're still feeling bad after three weeks, and especially if you're feeling worse, please don't ignore that. Make an appointment with your doctor.'

Struggling doesn't mean failing

One of the reasons why women don't report their negative feelings and mental health struggles is the worry around being labelled an 'inadequate' mother. Being a great mum is so important to us, and we're surrounded by messages about what that looks like. They add up to a picture of a serene, endlessly loving woman who's always engaged with her baby, and is always happy and fulfilled. She's allowed to be tired, perhaps a little ragged on a bad day, but nothing too dark or troubling. Otherwise, she's failing at her most fundamental task. Women fear being judged and found wanting, whether by other mums, our loved ones, the authority figures in our lives, the medical system or ourselves. Sometimes, that sense of failure can keep women from getting the help they desperately need.

Fortunately, that wasn't the case for Taylor Murray, but it easily could have been. Taylor is 32, has been married to her husband for eight years and has a three-year-old son. They now live in Cleveland, Ohio, but their son was born in New Jersey, where they moved towards the end of Taylor's second trimester. A month after they arrived, anxiety took hold of her.

'I had him in August and by late September I was in a complete spiral. My son was only sleeping 45 minutes at a time because he had really bad acid reflux, and my husband was working until three in the morning. I was on my own with the baby all the time. My body was craving sleep. I felt disconnected from reality and worried that I was actually going crazy. My husband encouraged me to talk to my healthcare provider and I was very upfront. I told her I was thinking about taking my own life. She said it was just baby blues, which really made me panic because I knew it was more serious than that.

'Then my sister, who's a nurse, came to visit. She took one look at me and pretty much said, "This isn't safe. We're going to take you and the baby to mom's." My husband sat me down and said, "You're not a bad mom, focus on getting yourself better and then we'll work everything else out." He drove us up two days later, on Halloween, and the baby and I spent nearly two months at my mom's place. She took care of him so I could sleep three or four hours uninterrupted. I was able to take tiny steps, coming back into the world. We got home about a week before Christmas. Everyone was a little shy around me. I was like, it's all right guys, I'm not gonna off myself on Christmas. But seriously, my support system saved my life. My husband sacrificed two months with his son so I could get better, and my mom, dad and sister cared for me when I couldn't care for myself.'

Taylor had never suffered from depression or anxiety until her pregnancy, though she had always had mood cycles around her period. 'I now know that I have PMDD, so I'm super sensitive to the hormone fluctuations in my body. In hindsight, pregnancy and giving birth sent me over the edge. My husband's support was crucial. He didn't once make me feel like I was crazy or failing; he treated the situation like a medical problem, plain and simple. The same with my family. I don't think I would have managed without that, especially since I felt let down when I went to my doctor.'

Taylor's support network stepped up when she needed it, which made all the difference for her. She's adamant that her village saved her life. But not every woman has a loving non-judgemental partner, a sister who's a nurse and parents who can take over in a crisis. That's why it's so important that we look for wide-ranging support and offer it to others whenever we have the capacity. Sharing stories about our moments of crisis helps to normalize them and remind ourselves that we are not failing when we struggle, and we are never alone. In fact, a crisis can be a catalyst for deep healing and long-term improvement in our mental health.

Having my little girl gave me the push I needed to get help. I want her to have healthy coping strategies and better mental health than I do. That's my focus now.

— Izzy C.-C., US

The Sticky Stuff:
Fed is best

We know that questions and worries about feeding
our baby can end up triggering deep distress for
many of us. There's way too much guilt, shame and
judgement attached to the issue of whether, when and
how to introduce formula alongside breast milk. Why
has this issue become such a minefield? And what can
you learn from other mums about how they've steered
their way through stress and self-doubt to a place
of calm?

In the last 30 years there has been a push by health
authorities all over the world for exclusive breastfeeding
until a baby is six months old. Women have taken up
the challenge. The vast majority try to breastfeed their
children – 88 per cent of new mothers in the UK initiate
breastfeeding, for example, with similar figures in the
States. And yet only 1 per cent of British babies are still
being exclusively breastfed by the time they reach six
months.

So many new mothers struggle with feeding.
Specifically, they struggle to breastfeed their baby as
much as they want to, or at all. This causes anxiety, guilt
and shame, and studies show this can have a massive
negative impact on women's emotional state and mental
health. Which makes sense, because there are few more
vital and emotive issues than how you feed your baby,
especially when you've been told, as many women have,
that breastfeeding is the most important thing you can

ever do for your child. If breastfeeding turns out to be impossible for you, as it is physiologically for some women, or you have to return to work when your baby is three months old, or it's just too damn hard so you start to supplement with formula, then it's hardly surprising that you're going to feel down on yourself and worried for your child.

We're not here to go into the pros and cons of breast, formula or a mixture of the two, feeding on demand or on a schedule. There's already a lot of information available on the subject. But there's also a lot of *mis*information and a whole heap of opinion, especially on social media and among family and friends. The pressure can feel enormous. 'What I see is that women who *have* been able to breastfeed still worry too much about feeding, and the women who weren't able to or decided not to worry and stress even more,' says Dr Lisa Folden, physical therapist and body image coach. 'Mothers are fielding other people's expectations, conflicting information and a lot of unnecessary guilt. The research on stress is clear: it hurts our bodies. It's more impactful than what we eat and how we move. Please, whatever your body is doing or not doing, express your feelings but don't adopt those feelings as your beliefs about yourself. Instead, tell yourself that you are doing a good job.' We hope those words land for you, and that hearing from other mums who've had a range of experiences with feeding their children brings some perspective and reassurance.

'I was adamant that I wanted to breastfeed, especially because I hadn't been able to deliver my son the way I'd hoped, but I really struggled. There was the pain and the cracked nipples and the trauma of his birth. One midwife in the hospital helped me to latch him but I only saw her once and I didn't have any other help from professionals. It was TikTok videos that helped. Someone mentioned the flipple technique and that seemed to click. We're now 11 months into breastfeeding exclusively and I'm so glad and grateful, but the first two weeks were awful and definitely contributed to my sense of failure.'

— Grace Williams, UK

'With my second child I did combi-feeding, so I breastfed and also did formula. I found it impossible to do exclusive breastfeeding when I also had a toddler running around. I know some people can manage that but I couldn't.'

— Kat Whittam, UK

'I was very self-conscious about my body and about breastfeeding in public. The women I met at my antenatal group were a really good support. Not all of them were breastfeeding but some of them were and it was nice to have company when I was out and about with the baby. They were so secure about it. They gave me a lot of confidence.'

— Nicole Arruda, UK

'Breastfeeding is all trial and error and it doesn't work for everybody. You know, I've tried a couple of times and it didn't work for me.'

— **Liesl Verzal, US**

'I didn't know much about breastfeeding before I had her and it's definitely been a challenge. I took a day-long class in my last week of pregnancy but now I think nothing could really have prepared me. It felt like it took so long for my milk to come in! It's hard to stay on top of eating and drinking yourself, while also tending to your baby. And when I get stressed my milk supply goes down. It's easy to get in a spiral of worry. You so badly want to feed your baby what she needs, but your body may have other plans.'

— **Jasmin Jefferies, US**

'Often it's all on the mother to deal with feeding a baby. It isn't like that for us because we are both the mothers, and my wife did not breastfeed. So we were both able to feed her and get up with her in the night. That made a world of difference.'

— **Marcia, US**

'I decided I wasn't going to breastfeed even before my son was born. I've always struggled with my mental health and I have an obsessive personality, so I knew that if I had problems with feeding I would be micro-focused on what was going wrong. I didn't want to risk it. Also, I wanted my husband to be as involved with the baby's care as me. I'm proud of myself for making that decision. In the end, Miller was born at 33 weeks, so he spent his first weeks in the neonatal unit, which meant I couldn't have breastfed him anyway.'

— Rachael Kall, UK

Whether you're feeling mildly nervous, anxious or desperate, please know that there are thousands of other mums out there struggling with those same thoughts and emotions, not to mention the extra burden of feeling bad about feeling bad. Give yourself the grace to take your feelings and symptoms seriously. Make space to talk to someone and ask them to help you access support. You can do this. And please, remember that coping with mental health problems doesn't make any of us weak or a failure. On the contrary, it makes us heroes. Let your light shine so the rest of the village can see you clearly.

In a nutshell . . .

Feeling overwhelmed is normal and nothing to feel ashamed about. It's perfectly fine to have days where you don't feel great and everything is hard. What are the small proactive steps you can take on days like that? Have you brushed your hair or got changed? Have you spoken to an adult? Have you picked up a book or watched some TV? Having easy strategies to meet your own needs is crucial.

Baby blues or postpartum depression? Baby blues kick in within days of giving birth and clear up within a couple of weeks. Postpartum depression and anxiety can begin before birth and any time up to a year afterwards. Symptoms of baby blues are mood swings, crying, sadness, irritability. Symptoms of postpartum depression and anxiety include hopelessness, severe mood swings, panic attacks, not being able to·bond with your baby, withdrawing from loved ones. If you've been feeling low for two consecutive weeks, it's getting worse, or you're thinking about harming yourself or your baby, seek professional support. You won't be judged or punished, and you certainly won't be the only one going through it.

Be honest about how you're feeling – with everyone. You can't get the help you need if you don't tell people how you really are. That means not sweeping problems under the rug. Shame, fear of judgement, internalized feelings of failure or anxiety about repercussions can all keep us silent, but if your distress is getting worse, don't wait until you feel terrible. Speak to a loved one or a healthcare professional and keep speaking until you find someone who hears you and can help you make a plan.

There are safe treatments available for breastfeeding mothers. Don't assume there's nothing that can be done. There is a wide range of safe and effective treatments available for perinatal mental health conditions, from specialist postnatal counselling to anti-anxiety, antidepressant and antipsychotic medication. There are also support groups for mums with mental health issues where you can meet fellow sufferers and hear how people have been able to recover.

CHAPTER 7

When am I supposed to
have a shower?

On troubleshooting, drudgery and crazy logistics

Having a newborn really boils life down to its essential activities: feeding, sleeping, cuddling and cleaning up – but even these basics can feel pretty challenging, as Jasmin Jefferies discovered. Jasmin is a single mum who lives in Atlanta, Georgia, with her 11-week-old daughter, who, in her words, is 'growing like a weed'. She says, 'My mom and dad have been with us for these first three months, which has made all the difference. I'm so grateful. They've been able to go get food for me and help out around the house, but there's so much to be done and of course their own priorities don't just vanish. Even with all their help, many things that were simple before having a baby are now *so* hard. I have to plan my showers or take one as soon as I get the opportunity. People say, *sleep when the baby sleeps*, but you can't because that's your moment to take that shower, clean the kitchen or do the laundry.'

Jasmin and her baby are both doing really well, which Jasmin puts down to having a family that believes in supporting one another. Her mother's side especially has always seen taking care of children and other vulnerable people as a duty, and a group activity. Jasmin's grandfather was brought up in foster care, 'so there are a lot of folks on my mom's side that aren't blood-related but I've always known them as my cousin, aunt, or uncle. We're there for each other through our ups and downs. I knew I was going to have the support I needed.' Even so, and despite her parents moving in, the practicalities of the first three months have been challenging . . .

'For the first month I slept downstairs on the sofa. I didn't even make it to bed. Going up and down the stairs felt like such hard work after the birth. I'm exclusively breastfeeding and it's been difficult, so I had my corner of the sofa all set up and it just felt easier to stay there, pretty much round the clock. That's been a surprise. How stuck in one spot you feel. I've developed something called "mother's wrist" which is like carpal tunnel syndrome. It began during pregnancy and it's getting worse now that I'm holding and carrying her. I saw my doctor last week and he suggested physical therapy sessions. But how am I going to find the time for that? I'm going back to work full-time in a few weeks and my folks are heading back to their place. I'm not sure how yet, but I'll have to find ways to manage.'

The first few weeks and months of motherhood open us up to all sorts of logistical challenges that Pre-Baby Us could never have imagined would be such a big deal. The shower question is one. So many women mentioned it when we asked them about the early days, usually in a tone of amazement that something so simple had become so *complicated*. Then there are the related questions, like 'When am I supposed to clean the house?' 'Why does it take so long to get out the door?' and 'How can one tiny baby make so many poopy diapers in one day?' There's a lot of rote labour, cleaning and washing involved as you and your family settle into a new life, and sometimes it feels as if you need at least four pairs of hands to get it all done. Especially if you have more than one kid. Add to that the constant feeding, the nap schedule and your own exhaustion and it can feel as if you're clocking in and out of shift work, 24/7.

Even if you don't opt for charts and schedules as Dr Zoya did for her twins, you might well find yourself wondering whether the key to a content baby and your own sanity lies in nailing the everyday micro-challenges of motherhood. 'Organization is key,' says Kat W. 'Having everything to hand makes nappy-changing a baby and a toddler in quick succession that little bit easier.' Vanessa R. from the US tackles the how-to-shower question head-on by making it her number-one priority. 'I list and prioritize tasks by importance. For me, it's a shower first. I need to feel clean so I can tackle everything else.'

But we all react differently to what poet Jess Urlichs calls 'the beautiful chaos of motherhood'. While some of us find it comforting and helpful to create structure and seek order, others prefer to welcome a messier version of reality. It can feel liberating to accept that the house will be less than immaculate because we have different priorities now, at least for a while. There's something to be said for accepting that caring for a baby is a full-time job. Doing that while trying to keep a perfect family home is going to stretch anyone's capacity, no matter how organized you are.

Stephani E., who lives in Montana in the US, recently took a part-time job as a server to boost the family income. She's at work while her husband is at home with their girls. There's a gleeful look in her eye when she says that he recently told her he finally understood why the house is messy after a day at home with the kids. 'I've always said the chores can wait because you can't do it all, and you don't get this time back. It was like he got it for the first time, but he had to actually live for himself the experience of not being able to meet all those demands.'

Many women have a certain idea of how maternity leave will pan out, especially if we're fortunate enough to be able to take an extended period off work. It can be difficult to imagine six months or a year of unstructured time, let alone what having a baby to look after entails. We might plan to take a language course, write a novel or at the very least keep an immaculate house and get back in shape. If activities like these feel right for you, fantastic. But please don't put pressure on yourself to 'achieve' certain goals. Kellie Leonard has some succinct advice for those of us who aim for perfection and struggle with giving anything less than 100 per cent of our efforts at all times. 'Your maternity leave is not a job you have to excel at. I want to tell women, no, you've had a baby, caring for the baby is enough for now. It's okay to share responsibilities and ask for help.' We couldn't agree more.

> *Remember to pause and really enjoy each stage with your baby and family. Don't worry so much about a messy house or keeping up with things. And be willing to ask for help. You will need it!*
>
> — **Isabella L., US**

Weird problems and the hunt for the perfect workaround

Alongside the work of caring for your baby and keeping the house and yourself at least clean *enough*, there's also all the 'worry work', the mental load of trying to fix problems and find solutions, whether that's soothing a colicky baby or figuring out whether he actually does have a dairy intolerance. As Deanna S. from the US put it, 'You end up searching for answers to questions you never thought you would need to ask, like, "What should my baby's poop look like?" or "What's the best nose cleaner for a baby?" You send yourself crazy trying to do the best for them when most times you are already doing just that.'

Some questions do need answers and some problems can be solved, but we agree with Deanna – you're already doing a lot. And not everything that feels like a problem has a solution, or perhaps not the kind that we assume. As Lizzie W. from the UK said, 'My breakthrough moment was realizing that there was actually no fix for the problem I'd been sending myself mad over.' Lizzie just could not figure out which order to do bedtime routines for her newborn and her toddler in, on the evenings when it was just her at home. 'I kept looking for the perfect solution, like if I feed her while I'm sitting by his bath then she'll be happy enough to be put down while I dry him off . . . Nothing worked. Someone always ended up screaming hysterically while I helped the other child. A friend with three older kids eventually said to me, "You can't fix this, so stop fretting. One of them is going to cry a little. And that's okay." It was such a relief to be given permission to stop trying. I calmed down after that and just got through it as gently as I could.'

There's always a balance to be struck. On the one hand it's important to have that shower and restock the nappy supply. On the other, most mums are already working round the clock to do everything they can as perfectly as possible, so perhaps giving ourselves permission to embrace being *good enough* would make life easier.

These early days are so work-intensive and hands-on that

they really prove the truth of the proverb about the village. But the people in your immediate village may have their own issues with capacity, or not know how to help. If you have a live-in partner, for example, they're likely to be struggling with adjustment to the new reality and sleeplessness as well. (There's more on tensions with partners over the division of labour in the chapter on relationships coming up soon. So many women tell us that having a cleaner or a partner who pulls their weight, or *both*, has become their ultimate fantasy.)

> Since I gave birth to my daughter, my sister and I have never been closer. This is her first niece. She doesn't want kids of her own, and she loves my daughter like she birthed her herself. The week after my C-section, she came over and helped me shower every day. I'll never forget it.
>
> **— Bethany B., UK**

If you were expecting a little more from your family or friends, you might be feeling disappointed and resentful. 'During the first few months of my daughter's life my friends seemed to vanish,' Becca A. from London told us. 'I didn't understand why they couldn't see that I was having a hard time. I thought it was obvious that I would have appreciated their company. All they had to do was come and hang out, make me a cup of tea. But now that I'm out of that phase I see it differently. You can't really know what's helpful for new parents until you've had a child yourself. A couple of my friends have had babies recently and I'm much bolder now that I've had my own. I'm, like, "Okay what do you need? Can I come over? Can I pick up some shopping or go to the pharmacy? Do you want me to hold the baby while you shower?"

Oh look, we've come full circle back to the dreaded shower question again . . .

Back off out of my baby bubble

Whether or not you want visitors during the first few weeks, with or without groceries and offerings of cake, is a highly personal matter. Resting up in a safe space is a priority for many women and lots of people talk about 'nesting' or settling into the 'baby bubble' so they can get to know their baby and learn the basics of looking after them. You might be craving security and privacy so you can rest, heal and adjust to your new reality. But it's different for all of us and will probably be different day to day for any one of us. Maybe, like Becca, you need peace and quiet for a few days or weeks and then find yourself desperate for a visit and a chat with an old friend. It can feel confusing, but try to be gentle with yourself. Being consistent just isn't really a thing at this point.

The baby bubble might be a physical space, especially if you live in your own home, but it's also an emotional zone, and new mothers can feel extremely protective of its boundaries. 'Family were sincerely trying to be helpful, offering to hold the baby or give him a wash so I could nap, but I physically didn't want to be separated from him,' said Jill Zucker, who lives in Columbus, Ohio, with her husband and almost-one-year-old son. 'That was a surprise: the extent to which I didn't want anyone else apart from his dad to hold him. Honestly, for the first two weeks I would have loved to be in a bubble, just me and the baby.'

And yet there's often a lot of pressure from close family and friends who want to meet your new child. When we asked the community about the challenges of the early weeks, so many women told us stories about how tough they found it to move beyond the baby bubble, or open it up to people. Jill told us that she was 'not ready to see anybody. My partner's family travelled to visit us and naturally they wanted to meet our son and help out, but I wanted to say, "Just give me these two months and then everybody can come visit." I needed rest and time to settle in with the idea that I was no longer alone. This little person who had been inside of me was now outside. What did that mean? So many things, right?'

Just as with Becca, Jill's needs ended up coming second to the wider family's, though in both cases their partners were skilled at managing the situation to make it easier. But these tensions over the baby bubble's boundaries can feel like skirmishes in bigger battles to come. They certainly were for Stephani Evans.

'Three weeks postpartum, my husband thought it was a great idea to go visit his parents. So we drove three hours to his dad's house. The baby was really unsettled and I was beginning to wonder whether she had a dairy intolerance. A few days later, we drove another hour and a half to his mom's house. Our daughter was crying all the time because her tummy was so painful. My mother-in-law inserted herself in ways that she shouldn't have. She had opinions about what was wrong with the baby, what she needed — bottle-feeding, basically — and at one point she actually took her from me and left the room. I told my husband, because I was crying at this point, "Go get our baby." So he left but when he came back, he didn't have her. He started trying to explain, "Well, my mom said . . ." I ran outside in my underwear and said, "Give her to me." She handed her over. But . . . taking a crying baby from a mom . . .' Stephani shakes her head, still disbelieving.

Stephani's experience was always going to be stressful but the fact that it happened just three weeks after she gave birth to her first child meant that she was particularly vulnerable. 'I hadn't wanted to go and visit them yet. It was too far and too soon. I was just settling into being a mother. Plus, I was worried about our daughter's stomach issues, so I was already tense.' No wonder Stephani felt criticized and judged by her mother-in-law.

And yet, Veronica Cisneros, who works with mothers on all aspects of their relationships, has an interesting perspective; one that might allow those of us who have had our boundaries crossed to find ways to respond rather than react. Veronica counsels trying not to view the behaviour that violated our boundary as an attack. 'Instead, try thinking, "This is what my mother-in-law looks like when she's panicked, when she's scared that I'm not protecting my kid. Her behaviour has nothing to do with me; it reflects her inability to regulate her own emotions." You'll then be in a better position to manage the situation and steer it the way you want it to go in the future.'

Having to do this emotional work to defend our needs and our boundaries when we're already stretched with adapting to motherhood can feel unfair. It's understandable if you want to duck those challenges for now and stay in the baby bubble until you feel less vulnerable. Gail Janicola, doula and new-mum mentor, advises women to think these issues through as part of their planning for birth and postpartum. 'You are absolutely allowed to set time limits. If you don't want people over immediately, you can say so. Do not be afraid to hurt people's feelings at this vulnerable and important time in your life. Try to talk about it calmly and clearly before you give birth, so people have time to process and understand what you're telling them. And if they don't understand . . . well, that doesn't have to be your top priority right now.'

Since becoming a mum I am less of a people-pleaser. I now have my own little person to please and care for, so everyone else's opinions and needs come second. I'm not scared to share that.

— Amber C., UK

The freedom to leave the house

When we asked our community what they missed about their life pre-children, the single biggest thing was freedom, closely followed by spontaneity. People talked about freedom to travel, pursue a hobby or up sticks and move house. To set their own course in life, without having to take anyone else's needs into account. Freedom is a big and glorious gift, for sure, but almost half of those who mentioned it talked about it in the context of a smaller, simpler life event: being able to just . . . *leave the house*. Alone. Whenever you want. Without packing a carry-on-sized bag of wipes and nappies and bottles and snacks. Get up and go, in one minute flat.

The leaving-the-house issue sums up mums' new reality, its constraints and its hidden labour. It speaks to the fact that, on some days, just getting out of the house to go to a doctor's appointment feels like a mission to Mars. Or the way it becomes a barrier to keeping up your social connections, especially if your friends invite you for coffee with half an hour's notice when it takes you that long to get out the door.

If your waking hours are currently spent battling to change all the nappies, soak all the poopy sleepsuits, sterilize the bottles, wipe down the kitchen surfaces, get in and out of the shower and then out the door, bag packed, in time for your appointment with the doctor, please know that we see you. We see your work, your patience, your care and your problem-solving. We see you figuring out how to be the best mum you can possibly be. Just promise us that you'll cut yourself some slack from time to time.

In a nutshell . . .

You are the best person to decide how and when you want to introduce people to your baby. This won't always go smoothly but it's great practice in boundary-setting – an essential skill in motherhood.

Try having an answer ready for when people say things like, 'Let me know if there's anything I can do.' That way you can ask for something that will actually make a difference such as a specific errand or chore, freeing you up to be with your baby or do something for yourself.

Not every problem has a solution but most of them eventually resolve themselves. If you're up against an impossible problem or the never-ending tasks are really getting to you, you could try channelling a Zen-like attitude by remembering that everything with children is temporary. Whether it's cluster feeding or tantrums, no phase lasts for ever. Being in the moment as much as possible can help you to enjoy the good times and observe that the bad times don't last long.

Let go of ideas of perfection as much, as often and as early as you can. This goes against the grain for many of us but it can make a big difference to your stress levels. Women already shoulder immense pressure about what we should be doing as partners, colleagues, friends. Motherhood adds a new set of expectations to that burden. Practise letting go of a few 'shoulds' so that you can focus on what actually matters to you.

PART THREE
The next few months

CHAPTER 8

Help, I need mum friends!

On isolation, loneliness and finding your people

There's a moment when you look around and it dawns on you . . . you're kind of on your own. Just you and your baby. For hours at a time. Maybe you're on maternity leave and are missing the busyness and chat of your workplace. Maybe your partner's parental leave has finished and they've gone back to their regular life. The initial flurry of excited visits and messages from friends and family has dried up. Life is quieter, at least in terms of your interactions with other adults, though your little one is probably making plenty of noise. You might be spending a lot of time on social media, trying to stay connected, which can come with its own problems – especially if you're comparing your experience of motherhood with other people's.

Rachael Kall, who's 36 and lives in Bolton in the UK with her husband, their five-year-old son and two kittens, is very honest about her lifelong feelings of loneliness and the acute isolation she felt as a new mum. 'I've struggled with loneliness and feeling socially out of place all my life. My mum died when I was 17 and, after that, my teenage friendships fell apart. I tried to make new friends, but it was always hard and there have been times when I've felt extremely alone in the world. Going into motherhood kind of confirmed that to begin with. My husband's a chef and works really long hours, so a lot of the time I was at home with the baby on my own. It's so isolating. You're just thrown into the midst of this chaos, with so much responsibility and nobody to share it with. My son was born at 33 weeks, before I'd even started antenatal classes, so I didn't meet people that way. When he came out of hospital, I started taking him to music and play classes but he was at a completely different development stage from other babies. I ended up thinking there was something wrong with him, which made me feel even lonelier. That was probably the low point.

'Then I decided I had to take motherhood as an opportunity to reinvent myself. I began to organize mums' meet-ups online, which felt less scary. I found one great local friend who's still part of my life, and that was a turning point. I organized social events at my son's nursery and then made another group of friends at his school. I had to push myself to go out and try to connect with people, but each time I did, it gave me the confidence to take the next step. I now have the most amazing bunch of friends – they're everything I ever dreamed of – but I still remember how awful the early days were. I thought it was just me who was struggling but when I began to speak openly with people, I discovered it's lonely for everyone.'

Loneliness and isolation in early parenthood are incredibly common – almost half of new mothers in the UK report feeling lonely often or always according to a 2016 study by the British Red Cross. Some studies suggest as many as 90 per cent of mums feel lonely at times during the first year of their child's life. That's hardly surprising when 38 per cent of mums spend eight hours a day alone with their child. Unfortunately, feeling lonely is not just unpleasant; it has devastating effects on our physical and mental health. Human beings, even the most introverted or socially awkward of us, are social creatures. We need contact with other people. Feeling lonely for prolonged periods can be as damaging as smoking 15 cigarettes a day, according to a 2015 study carried out by Julianne Holt-Lunstad at Brigham Young University. The effects of loneliness are also felt more acutely by certain groups, especially young mums aged 16 to 24 and immigrant parents who don't have full fluency in the local language.

> *As a young mum, it's difficult when your friends are all moving on and having fun while you're at home looking after a baby. It can be challenging to accept that they don't understand what it's like. It feels very lonely.*
>
> **— Mackenzie K., UK**

The thing about feeling lonely is that it makes everything else harder. If you're already battling low mood, anxiety and lack of confidence, then sitting on your own with the dirty nappies and a screaming baby is not going to do you any favours. But as we know, it's not always easy to get out of the house, accept invitations from friends or motivate yourself to find new connections. You're tired, the baby needs to nap, you haven't got anything to talk about, or perhaps you've got a lot to talk about but it's all a bit *negative*, so it feels easier to stay on the sofa.

We get it, but we're here to tell you that having mum friends is mission-critical at this point in your life. Top priority. Your potential friends are the people you can build a village with, and they *are* out there. As Rachael says, however lonely you feel, you are definitely not alone. Look at those stats – we're all in the same boat.

The honest guide to making mum friends

So how to go about it? There are really two questions here: firstly, where are all the other mums hanging out? And secondly, how can you force yourself to get chatting with them if you're a) shy, b) anxious or c) have already tried to make friends without any luck and are feeling extra nervous?

For the first question, the internet is your friend. Seek out local mum and baby groups, classes and hangouts in leisure centres, libraries and community spaces. There will be more options in cities than in rural areas, but there is bound to be *something* going on. Or flip the question and ask yourself what you like doing and whether there is a bunch of mums who are already doing it. This has worked well for lots of women in our community. Stephani E. moved to Montana partly because she loves outdoor activities, so when she was looking for friends for herself and her daughters, she went online. She found a group for mums who liked to hike with their kids, which led her to a woman who was into cross-country skiing who became a friend and introduced her to a bunch of women who also love rock climbing. They take their kids along with them and take it in turns to climb.

The second question is probably the trickier one. The emotional and social challenges of striking up a conversation, making a connection and turning that into a friendship can feel huge. But here, we have your back, because every single mother has been where you are now. For a start, making mum friends, just like dating, is a numbers game. Persistence is key. You might invest in a relationship, think you're getting somewhere and then get ghosted. It's tough but it happens. It can help to remember that everyone else is also struggling with their energy and capacity. As usual, a bit of compassion and trying not to take things too personally will make it easier to figure out whether a supportive text is all the other person needs to hear to fix that coffee date, or whether you need to move on.

I have not been able to make the friendships that I would hope for but that is my own doing. I find it hard to keep up with messaging new people and keeping up with surface-level conversation. I have tried a few times and ended up accidentally ghosting people without meaning to.

— Louise C., US

Don't be afraid to leave a group if you don't like its vibe. It's a good idea to give any new group a couple of chances before you decide that it's not for you. But you don't need to keep going to story time at the library for months on end if nobody ever chats. Try somewhere else.

Or do it yourself! Is there a local cafe you like to hang out in? Would you like to meet mum friends there? How about setting up a super-informal mums' coffee morning? It could be as simple as asking the cafe owner, putting a sign in the window and posting on your socials and any local community boards. Then get ready to chat . . . If only one other person turns up the first time, do it again and we practically guarantee there will be more people the second time.

Peanut Professional Darcel Being, who is based in Florida and coaches mums to live the wholehearted lives they long for, has a simple and inspiring route map to finding your people. 'First, what's your vision? That's not "finding mums who are fun". What does that look like? Get specific. Mums who love to garden? Great. Then, what value are you going to bring to this group of gardening mums? What can you give or do to make this group thrive? Set up a group chat, meet up in a park, host an online chat about gardening with your kids? Fantastic. Finally, use your voice. Tell people about it. Do that often enough and you cannot fail to find your people.'

If in-person socializing isn't your thing, look for a supportive online community or make one yourself. That's what Kerry T. did when she was finding it hard to connect with local mums. 'I'm British in America and there are definitely cultural differences at play. Plus, I'm a geek, and I eventually realized that what I really wanted was a mums' group on Discord. So I set it up. Now there are 200 of us hanging out, playing video games, running movie nights and bingo nights. There's a baking club, a book club, we do competitions. I basically made my mum village online.'

Don't give up

What if it still isn't working? What if you've been looking for ages and you still feel lonely? Perhaps you've tried to join groups that have felt unwelcoming and given up. Maybe you've just never quite clicked with anyone, or haven't been able to keep a friendship as your kids grow. These situations can feel scary and very shaming, as if there's something wrong with us. Lurking beneath our surface-level worries, whether they're about discovering we have nothing in common with the mum we'd hoped to befriend, or that our kids will be misbehaving while theirs are good as gold, lie fears of being judged or rejected and feeling shamed. These in turn often tap into older social fears of not being able to break into a clique, or find our own tribe.

Please know that it happens to so many people. Peanut Professional Deb Cichon is a mental health counsellor based in New York City who works with mothers on their friendship and relationship difficulties. She says that women come to her saying that they've come across behaviour that 'reminds them of high school. They've found groups that felt gossipy or competitive and other mums who are judgemental and cliquey. This can be very distressing, but I've found that talking about these experiences relieves some of the negative feelings. It helps to hear that practically everyone struggles, but also that most of us do find our people in the end, if we keep looking.'

Deb is speaking from experience here. 'That was definitely the case for me. I have three kids and I didn't have any luck with mom friends after my first child. I was 25 and felt pretty rejected by the older moms I met. I found that very hard and it played into difficulties with mental health. It's been very different with my second and third children and I see the dramatic difference in my improved wellbeing. I would say to anyone who's struggling, don't give up. And if you have postpartum anxiety, please talk to other moms about it. It's so common; you will find people to bond with.'

Kirsty Williams, who lives in Westwood, Massachusetts, has two children and bears witness to the wisdom of Deb's perspective. She didn't manage to find friends after her first child but has gone on to build a flourishing social life. She now helps other mums to find each other through her voluntary work in her local community.

'We moved to the area when I was pregnant with my first child, and I joined the local Mothers Forum so that I'd have a network of people. I went to some play sessions with my daughter and tried really hard to make connections, but it was very challenging. I had postpartum anxiety and that meant my energy was pretty low, but I didn't feel I could talk to anyone about it. The anxiety and the lack of friends played off each other and made me feel worse. It was hard to make friendships that stuck, and I found that really dispiriting. Even when my eldest went to nursery and then school, friendships felt like they were coming and going; it was a revolving door.'

Kirsty has social anxiety and found that the isolation of the early motherhood years made it worse. After she had her second daughter, she decided she had to do something. 'I knew I had to get out of my comfort zone. I went back to the Mothers Forum and volunteered to take on a role working with new members, welcoming them and integrating them into the group. My motivation was to do something for women who were in a similar position to the one I found myself in. That framing helped me to actually go and do it. It's been wonderful because now I have the social network I always wanted, and I feel I'm giving something back to my community.'

Your first steps towards building your own village don't need to be huge. It's fine to push on your comfort zone only when you're ready, as Kirsty did. We hope that you, like Kirsty and Rachael, find that one friend leads to another and before long you've got your group, your gang, your people in place around you. This is the village in action – a mutually supportive network built on understanding and kindness that brings benefits to everyone who takes part.

In a nutshell . . .

Feeling lonely is not your fault and it doesn't mean you're failing. In fact, it's very common and reflects the lack of support from the wider village. There's no need to feel ashamed or guilty. Instead, look for every opportunity to connect with other people, especially other mums. They're probably feeling exactly the same as you and would welcome it if you reached out. If it doesn't work out the first time, try not to take it personally, simply move on and try again.

Could you start a group or a meet-up? Or could you support someone else's? It might be as simple as setting up a WhatsApp group for mothers on your street, inviting two or three people to join and spreading the word. One micro group on Peanut started exactly like that; now it has 30 members who meet for weekly mum and baby picnics in a local park. If you don't have the energy to start something or participate right now, but you appreciate someone else's efforts, tell them. We can all do more to encourage each other, and small connections can be picked up again when you do have the bandwidth.

Be honest about what you're looking for with yourself and others but accept that it might take trial and error to work out exactly what that is. A particular aspect of your experience might act as glue for a friendship. Some women bond when their babies are on neonatal wards, for example. But it's also good to keep an open mind about where friends may or may not come from. In the same way that motherhood alone is not necessarily enough to bring people together, neither are other aspects of your identity. Some same-sex parents find it valuable to join groups for same-sex parents, for example; others prioritize finding local friends with babies the same age. It's fine to try out different groups and tactics, so long as you're open and kind with all the people you meet.

CHAPTER 9
Do I hate my in-laws?

*On different values, expectations and
battles over baby-led weaning*

Adriana is from Brazil and lives in Lisburn, Northern Ireland, with her husband and their two-year-old daughter. They met in London but decided to move back to her husband's hometown when she fell pregnant. Adriana's in-laws were enthusiastic about becoming grandparents and said they were happy to help with childcare, so that the couple, who both do shift work, could carry on working. Unfortunately, the situation quickly turned difficult.

'I got the feeling that my parents-in-law did not actually want to help us,' says Adriana. 'I imagined that it would be a lovely thing for them to spend time with their first grandchild, but they seemed to view it as a task that we were trying to push on them. Even before I went back to work, if I was sick and asking my mother-in-law to be with our daughter for the day so I could rest, she would refuse. Her attitude seemed to be, "I managed four kids by myself. And you cannot even manage one."

'It got really bad when I decided to take a home-based job working online rather than going back to the factory. They refused to help with any childcare at all, saying I didn't need help since I was at home. I found it so upsetting. The job was almost full-time hours and I wanted to do it, so I tried to make it work, but it was hard. When my husband's sister had her own baby, the reaction and the treatment was very different. Nothing was too much trouble. I felt I was being treated completely differently. It was upsetting for my husband as well. He felt it very deeply. For me, the contrast with my family in Brazil made it even more painful. Over there the extended family is a big thing and grandparents are generally happy to help out. It's not a job, it's a pleasure to be part of caring for their grandchildren. So perhaps some of these difficulties are cultural. I don't know.'

Tension with family members crops up all the time for women still navigating the new territory of motherhood. Maybe you'd like more support, as was the case for Adriana, or a little more personal space, like Marcia, whose story is coming up soon. Perhaps there are open disagreements with your parents or in-laws that have escalated into arguments. Or it could be an unspoken mood, a snide comment or endless unasked-for advice.

If you do have support from family, whether from parents, grandparents, siblings or in-laws, then it's pretty likely that by now you've had a few tetchy words, possibly even rows over caring for your baby or your approach to family life. After all, you've been tired for months now and your baby still needs you round the clock. Your patience gets used up dealing with your child's needs. There might not be much left over for your mum if she never stops telling you how different it was in her day. The first few years of motherhood are a perfect breeding ground for conflict with your nearest and dearest. Take a deep breath and let us help you to feel a little better about it.

What's really going on when you
fight with family?

Adriana and her husband felt deeply let down because they thought his parents were enthusiastic about being hands-on grandparents and the reality turned out to be different. They believed they had an understanding, but somewhere along the line, the communication had broken down.

Negotiations with family always depend on goodwill, clear communication, empathy, understanding, flexibility, honesty and commitment, but that's especially true when it comes to the people you hope will support you and your family at this challenging time. The stakes are high and tensions and resentments are never far from the surface. Not every situation revolves around a big question like childcare, but even seemingly smaller issues often tap into deeper fears and old insecurities. For Adriana, the conflict was especially painful because she perceived it as unfair – she was not being treated the same as her sister-in-law – and also because it underlined the difference with her own parents and made her miss them even more.

There are so many emotional currents swirling around when we get into difficulties with family, but not all of them are really anything to do with us. Different generations have different realities, and when two or more family groups come together around a new child, interactions are likely to be complex, especially if there are opposing values and other cultures at play. Lots of people tell us about difficulties over how to discipline children, for example, or grandparents favouring one set of grandchildren over another. Disagreements and resentments can cause friction throughout the wider family.

Sometimes, the most helpful thing you can do is try to step back and see the bigger picture from as many points of view as possible, though it's not always easy to be empathetic when tempers are running high. Adriana has been able to do this with support from a therapist, who has helped her to see that certain expectations are affecting how she and her husband view his mother's behaviour. 'Even when we're adults ourselves, we expect perfection from our mothers,' says Adriana. 'But my mother-in-law is a human being who has a different relationship with her daughter than her son. She feels like giving more support to her, as they have a stronger bond. I'm learning not to expect and not to compare how my in-laws treat us. My husband is still processing. I try to help him with that.'

Sometimes, volatility can lead to vulnerability and greater closeness and understanding. One UK-based mum told us that her relationship with her sister, which is very close but prone to the occasional upset, has allowed her to figure out other more challenging family dynamics. The two of them talk openly about their own tensions and also help each other to see different interpretations of their parents' and respective in-laws' behaviour.

Personal space, well-meaning intrusions and compromise

Even when it's welcome, family support usually comes with baggage. For Marcia, her wife's relationship with her birth family can feel overwhelming. 'While we were going for fertility treatment, everyone was on top of us. They would call immediately after every appointment. I'm much more independent than my wife but she is super close to her family and really needs that support system. We live in the same town as them, which is great in terms of practical help but also complicated. Sometimes I feel she doesn't have any boundaries with her folks. Recently I have said that between six and eight at night, we are not going to answer the phone. We're all learning what everyone needs and where to draw boundaries.'

Compromise and trade-offs are inevitable when it comes to managing wider family relationships. (And yes, this is yet more emotional labour that will likely fall on you.) Sierra C. from the US told us about her experience of getting into and out of a stand-off with her mother-in-law. 'She was fiercely critical of our decision to do baby-led weaning when my son was six months old. She told us he was going to choke on his food and said that she was only going to feed him purées because she couldn't stand by and watch us endanger our son. She made it all about her own anxieties. We ended up letting her give him purées simply because we were desperate for childcare. She constantly tries to parent my child and questions my parenting choices. It's debilitating but we have to make it work.'

My parents are too busy in their retirement to help regularly. It feels like I'm bothering them to watch my toddlers so that I can go to a doctor's appointment and actually hear what the doctor is saying. It's so disheartening. It's actually too raw to talk about.

— Danielle B., Canada

Defusing the disagreements

Baby-led weaning seems to be a touchstone issue for inter-generational disagreement. The advice has changed drastically in the space of a generation, so older relatives often assume that we will wean our baby from four months by giving them purées, rather than from six or seven months using baby-led weaning. Cue all sorts of confrontations, meltdowns and accus-ations. These rows can feel awful, even if we know that our mum or mother-in-law is simply acting out of concern and is telling us what was 'true' in her day. The challenge to our sense of being a loving and competent mother can feel like an attack and end up deepening tensions with wider family.

A similar sticky point is tummy time, which provoked a pointed exchange of views between Kerry T. and her mother-in-law. 'She insisted it was hurting my son's neck and told me not to do it. I said, "I'm an early years teacher and it's actually very beneficial." There have been a lot of comments like that from my mum as well as my in-laws. I can't help but take them personally. I think what helps is that I don't react in the moment. I try to keep calm and just explain, even though I'm so mad on the inside. Then I follow up with information over text message. My mother-in-law has always accepted what I've said fairly quickly, which is great. My mum takes a little longer. I usually end up saying things like, "Ways of doing things have moved on." Then she calms down.'

What else might help? The usual tough-to-do behaviours that make all relationships function a little more smoothly: things like clearly and calmly explaining your boundaries, trying to respond rather than react, looking at a situation from the other person's perspective. (We know. You probably don't want to hear this if you've just had a fight with your father-in-law over not washing his hands after smoking a cigarette and before he picks up your baby, which is what happened to one person from our community.)

> *My co-parent's family posted photos of our newborn son on social media before I did, and without my consent. This particularly upset me as I did not want my child on social media. My co-parent told his family to remove the pictures immediately and insisted they ask me if they want to share anything. It's never happened again.*
>
> **— Sarah V., UK**

It can be hard to know when we might be able to alter the behaviour that's driving us mad, by setting a boundary for example, and when it's more realistic to simply manage our own reactions. Veronica Cisneros helps people who are struggling with relationships to focus on what they *do* have control over, which often boils down to their own emotions. 'We'd love to change our mother-in-law and write her script for whenever she talks to us,' Veronica says with a smile, 'but we really can't.'

Shifting out of what Veronica calls 'the blame game' is tough and takes practice but can be rewarding in the long term. 'I noticed that once I really started working on my own insecurities, a lot of my behaviours shifted and my relationships felt less stressful,' she says. 'I did that by using a three-step process to observe what I was bringing to a situation. Everyone can do this. Firstly, identify what's coming up for you in terms of your thoughts. They might be, "I'm not a good enough mother. I'm never going to be good enough." Are you using words like "always" and "never"? Are you in a state of constant comparison? Next, what is the emotion attached to that? Are you feeling resentful? Are you feeling frustrated? Are you feeling overwhelmed? And then, how does your body respond? With tense shoulders or a knot in your stomach? Being able to observe these three elements in yourself – your thoughts, emotions and physical reactions – gives you a little bit of distance on the situation. That offers an opportunity for you to respond through problem-solving instead of reacting according to your frustrations or resentments.'

It's good life advice, even if it might not always feel possible when you're battling your mum over weaning your baby while picking cucumber sticks off the kitchen floor. Again. Good luck, Mama. You're not alone.

In a nutshell . . .

Figure out what matters to you first. When you feel confident and calm about your decisions and priorities it's easier not to react to any provocations from family. Look for support from a partner or a friend to sanity check your thinking and build up your self-confidence. That will make it easier to ride through tricky situations without escalating them.

Appreciate the support you do have. It's easy to dwell on what's driving you mad or what you don't have. It's hard but worthwhile to be grateful for any relationships that *are* meaningful and supportive. If you're envious of people whose parents are more hands-on than yours, for example, that's understandable but not helpful. Who else might be able to help out? Maybe there's an opportunity to deepen a different relationship, with an aunt and uncle or your sister-in-law.

'Good enough' relations with family might be the most realistic goal. Can you envisage what 'good enough' would look like for you? Sometimes it means taking a long-term perspective. Sometimes it means keeping parents or other family members at an emotional distance. Perhaps you want your child to know the wider family but accept that close relations are not going to happen. It can be liberating to stop expecting or hoping for more than what your family is able to provide.

Not every situation or dynamic can be resolved or improved. Only you can know the difference between a tricky relationship that's worth working through and one that requires you to set protective boundaries or break away from completely.

CHAPTER 10

How on earth does work fit into all this?

On finances, fulfilment, guilt and
what we all have in common

Destinie Guzman lives in New York City with her daughter, who is 18 months old. They're currently living with Destinie's grandmother, but she's hoping they will be rehoused soon. Destinie works as an associate in retail stores and has found it frustrating and exhausting trying to strike a balance between her need to work and her desire to be with her daughter. The situation has been made more difficult by the fact that she recently split from her daughter's father, and she's concerned that her grandma is becoming too frail to do childcare every day.

'I went back to work when my daughter was three months old. I didn't want to, but we needed an income. My ex-partner stayed at home with her and I worked a 35-hour week in a fashion retail store, from 2 p.m. to 9 p.m. five days a week, sometimes more. I found it so tough to be away from her and I was exhausted all the time. I would ask the managers if they could be a little flexible to accommodate me, let me switch a shift if I needed to, but they weren't understanding. I hated missing all that time with her and when I left work I would have to go home and take over from my ex. It was way too much.

'Just after she turned one, I quit that job and for the last few months we've been back living with my grandma to save some money on rent. I've prioritized spending time with my daughter. We've made some friends and been on a few days out. I'm spending the money I earned back then on fun things for us to do, like go to the zoo. At the end of the summer I'll look for another job. Maybe I'll have to put her in daycare so I can work more hours. I just hope I can find something that gives me a little more balance between working enough to make a living and actually being with her.'

Destinie's experience exposes the brutal reality of trying to combine employment and motherhood, especially when your support network is fraying. She works in a low-paid sector in one of the most expensive cities in the world and in a country where there is no statutory maternity leave. She ended up struggling to make ends meet and dealing with poor mental health. Destinie has been worrying about finding and keeping work ever since her child was born and, though she is calm and cheerful when she speaks, the strain is clear when she shakes her head as she tells her story.

Mothers all over the world face tough choices over how, when and whether to return to paid employment outside the home. Even where the state does provide maternity pay, the amount won't necessarily cover living costs unless it's topped up by provision from an employer – and employers vary hugely in how generous they are. For women who were unemployed before they got pregnant or who work freelance and don't have any workplace benefits, the shortfall can feel impossible to manage. Without financial support from family, insecurity for mother and child is the result.

Then there's the childcare problem. Decent, reliable childcare is hugely expensive in many countries and demand outstrips supply. Families may or may not be willing to help, and as we've seen, differing expectations can cause tensions. For those women who want or need to be employed, the logistics can feel daunting and the reality overwhelming.

Over the last 30 years, working mums' struggle to do and have 'it all' has become a cliché without a solution. It's still driving millions of women all over the world slightly insane. When we asked mums about challenges in the first couple of years of motherhood, so many of them were related to tension between these two responsibilities. Many of us need to work in order to make money to support our family. Many of us also *want* to work because our professional status is important to us. But of course we also want to be with our children. As all working mamas know, that means juggling all the time, which is exhausting.

Mums who choose to stay at home with their children tell us about a variety of motivations, from feeling it's their most important role to nerves around the quality of childcare and its prohibitive cost. Their choice also comes loaded with pressure and judgement from others. It can feel as if everyone has an opinion, from friends and loved ones to the influencer mums on TikTok.

Women's choices about work, career, ambition and looking after their families too often turn into a wedge issue in the culture war, which can make an already challenging question even tougher to think and talk about, let alone figure out. Dozens of Peanut users told us they worried about going back to work versus staying at home. They worried about making the right decision for their child, themselves and their family but also about not being able to cope with the double pressure, the sense of failing at everything, the guilt and being judged a bad parent. Planning how to combine employment and motherhood is daunting and, whatever you choose, your decisions are likely to come with a serving of guilt, confusion and possibly resentment.

So whether you're currently weighing up your possibilities or already have a plan, whether you're heading back to work when your baby's a few months old or settling in for a longer mat leave, we know that this issue is likely to be on your mind and stressing you out. Let's break it down.

What if it doesn't feel like a choice at all?

When you're trying to figure out what's possible, what's practical and what's worthwhile in terms of compromise and sacrifice, it can feel like you're juggling so much that the very idea of choice is laughable. What are the chances that what works for you, your child, your family and your boss will align? The juggle feels particularly difficult when your children are still babies. Some of the logistical challenges of caring for a baby while working outside the home can feel like a sick joke. How on earth are you supposed to exclusively breastfeed until your baby is six months old, for example, if you're back at work from 12 weeks postpartum?

Kori C. from the US told us that she couldn't square that particular circle. 'I went back to work part-time three months after I gave birth, but my baby wouldn't take a bottle and only wanted to be breastfed. It was too hard on him, me and the people watching him, so ultimately I had to quit. Now I'm a stay-at-home mom (SAHM) who is working on my own small business.'

Kori has found a solution to her dilemma, but working mums of infants are battling massive challenges. We hear from mums about pumping milk in office restrooms to take home at the end of the day, and months of discomfort, exhaustion and overwhelm as they grit their teeth and keep trying to reconcile the almost impossible demands of being a mum to a baby while also being an effective employee.

That sense of trying and failing to do the impossible eases up for many women as their children grow and everyone settles into new routines. But for some people it doesn't get easier. Helen B. lives in Malawi and has a toddler. She went back to her full-time teaching job when her child was six months and hated it. 'I was so tired all the time. I had no energy to be a great mum when I got home but I wasn't being very good at my job either. I made the difficult decision to leave and was criticized by the director of the school for putting my family first. I am still upset about it, even though it has been almost a year.'

The varying costs of childcare mean that while working is a financial obligation for some women, it's a financial impossibility for others, causing frustration and sadness for those who desperately want to make a particular choice and can't afford to. One US-based mum told us that now that she has two children, work is no longer an option. That's having an impact on her finances, her relationship with her husband and her wellbeing.

Damned if we do, damned if we don't

We've already talked about how motherhood presents us with many problems that lack solutions. Some of them feel like they should be simple but really aren't, such as taking a shower when you have a newborn. Some, like how to have a baby and a job, are so complex that it's kind of obvious we won't find the perfect answer. And yet that doesn't take away the pain of having to try.

Whatever compromise we eventually go with, it seems we'll be feeling guilty about it. Guilt runs like a red thread through women's discussion of their choices around employment and caring for their kids. Kathy H. from the UK sums up many women's anguish: 'I had to go back to work when she was 15 weeks old. Now I work full-time, I struggle to pay the nursery fees and I feel so guilty. I just want to be with her.' But stay-at-home mums also feel guilty. Many people tell us they feel bad for not contributing financially when they see their family struggling.

Mums spend years looking for the best possible solution to the work dilemma, tweaking their approach as their children grow up or their circumstances change. Women are endlessly inventive, seeking out new opportunities and sectors. Sometimes this means they hit on a solution that feels satisfying for them and their family. Sometimes it underlines their frustration at the whole damn juggle. 'I returned to work when my first son was six months old, having changed my career so I could work remotely full-time,' said Elizabeth K. from the US. 'It isolated me so much from other people that I lost my self-identity *and* I was still missing time with my son. I ended up changing careers again to work in an office. I kept changing careers until I found an office culture and career path that was fulfilling enough for me to justify the time away from my children.'

The worry, guilt and ambivalence that come along with the whole exhausting juggle can end up eating away at your confidence and happiness, creating tensions with loved ones and undermining your sense of self. Kylie H. from the US says, 'I am a full-time working mom and I'm always worrying about whether I'm doing things right or whether I'm doing things enough.'

The guilt that virtually all mothers feel, irrespective of their choices around work in and outside the home, is one of Dr Lisa Folden's key themes. She insists that the only solution to our guilt is to resist the impossible and toxic ideals of modern motherhood. Whether that's the self-sacrificing martyr-mother who is always happy to put her family's needs first, or the perfect hybrid mum who bosses it at work but never misses bedtime, we need to recognize them for what they are: unrealistic fictions that keep us feeling inadequate and unhappy. 'Motherhood is important but that doesn't mean we need to take it so seriously, or that it's the only important thing about us. We are all much more than mothers. I want moms to be comfortable setting boundaries and not feeling bad about it. Whether it's to protect your wellbeing or your work priorities, do not feel bad. Do not feel guilty or ashamed. I don't believe those feelings ever breed anything positive.'

Veronica Cisneros would say amen to that. She coaches women who are pursuing their careers while being mothers, and women who've opted to care for their children full-time. She says that although the day-to-day difficulties can feel different, the underlying emotions are very similar. 'There's a lot of guilt and resentment. The women wearing many different hats have often compromised themselves over and over again, trying to fulfil all the family's needs while still being a perfect employee or boss. The full-time carer moms also feel compromised and undervalued. It's easy for moms to lose themselves and end up terribly guilty and hugely resentful. Feeling guilty is no fun but resentment is a true killer of relationships and peace of mind. I help people regulate their emotions and process their resentments through honest conversations, including with themselves.'

Work, motherhood and identity

The conversation about mothers who work is often insufficiently honest and framed in simplistic ways. It either glosses over the economic reality that many mothers have no choice but to work, or sets women up in binary opposition – earth mothers who love to stay at home versus career women prioritizing their status in the public realm over their children. And yet so many women have much more complex and shifting feelings about work and motherhood. It's rarely a simple choice between the two, or a straightforward matter of gains and losses. Feelings and opinions change as we move through matrescence. There can be surprises along the way as we find our priorities shifting.

Sometimes it's a relief not to feel obliged to work so hard, endlessly putting in late hours and sacrificing our own well-being. Motherhood can offer an opportunity to take care of ourselves as well as our child. Many women in our community talk about being workaholics before they became parents, and relish asking themselves what they really need and want from life. If you're fortunate enough to have options, it can feel like a privilege to be able to pause adult life's rush and ask yourself big questions about your purpose and values.

Some women choose to work in the home, looking after their children's welfare and development full-time and perhaps homeschooling them. Others commit to careers, often sacrificing time with family and their own short-term wellbeing because the payback will eventually be worthwhile when they land their dream job.

Ambition is still seen as being incompatible with motherhood by many employers. It's also a challenge to our sense of self if we have to rethink what ambition looks like once we're mothers, as Chi Okafor discovered. Chi lives in Chicago, Illinois, with her Nigerian-American husband and their two sons, who are six and three. She has always been a very career-driven person. 'Growing up in Nigeria, I had grand plans to be a VP in a big corporation. I moved to the US when I married and worked for years in financial services, which I loved but knew was not compatible with family life. After my first son was born, I took a part-time position in finance. After my second, I did my MBA and planned to pivot into consulting. I knew that it was also a demanding sector, but I was hellbent on doing it. I would go for job interviews and ask about life for working mums and was always told the company was supportive, but I knew that might not be the case for the junior role I would be taking.'

Chi was nervous about whether she could combine a fast-paced job in a new sector with parenthood, but she couldn't imagine any alternative. 'So I took a summer internship at a strategy consultancy. It didn't work out. My mum came to take care of the kids and I hardly saw them all summer because I was working such long hours. My son got sick and there was zero understanding. It was enough to show me that I needed to re-evaluate my choices.'

Not just her choices but also her understanding of being an ambitious and successful woman. 'Some part of me felt like a failure,' Chi admits. 'I worried that I would be settling if I opted for a traditional 9–5 role, but I also knew that was the realistic plan. I'm now working full-time in finance. I'm in the office three days a week and working from home the other two. I leave at 5 p.m. to pick up my kids and then finish any outstanding work in the evening. I'm really happy with my new role. Surprised to be this happy with it! It's a tough choice to rethink what ambition means to me for now, a sacrifice in some ways, but I am so grateful that I get to spend the time with my children. That makes it all worthwhile.'

The Sticky Stuff:
Paid versus unpaid work

Firstly, we have to caveat this by saying that all labour is work, whether it's inside or outside the home. What people are most often referencing when they say 'working mum' is someone who is undertaking *paid* work outside of the home. For the sake of this debate, we're using the same terminology.

There are few more polarizing issues than the one that pitches working mums and stay-at-home mums against one another. It should be an entirely personal matter, especially since it's often less a choice than a necessity, but somehow it's ended up feeling ideological. This seems to be especially true in the US, where many members of our community have found themselves caught up in judgemental and critical conversations with other mums – but it's an issue everywhere. As ever, we're not here to debate the pros and cons, much less tell you what to do, only to show you how other women have thought through their choices and dealt with any friction in social situations.

While Chi was on her first maternity leave, she found that there were definitely two camps of mums: those who were planning to return to paid work and those who weren't. Or rather, those who were planning to pay for childcare and those who weren't. 'I had a friend who was a SAHM. When it was time for me to start work, she made a comment in passing, like "I can't imagine putting my kids in daycare. I couldn't do that to them . . ." I don't think she thought through what she was saying and probably didn't mean anything by it, but I struggled with hearing that. It made me doubt myself and my choices. Then I realized I just hadn't yet found a group of mums I could really be myself with. I'd like to have honest conversations about these choices and normalize all options rather than shaming each other. It's important to build communities that welcome working mums as well. So many events and playdates are fixed for working hours. It would be great to think about mums who can't make them and try to be as inclusive as possible.'

Inclusivity or lack of it in mums' groups is an issue that comes up a lot in our community. There's a lot of anxiety about being judged and found wanting on any number of issues, of which the 'working' mum versus SAHM is just one. But it's one of the biggest. And yet, Veronica's insight that working and stay-at-home mums have far more in common – same guilt, overwhelm and frustration – than they have differences, might just be the reminder we need to go beyond the surface with each other.

'These women are both in this struggle, mirroring each other,' says Veronica. 'I see envy on both sides. The working mom envies the stay-at-home mom who knows everything about her kid, and the stay-at-home mom envies the working mom her success, her identity and her contribution to the world. Sometimes the envy translates into mutual criticism. This is a zero-sum game built on insecurities and not having enough clarity on what we value and want to pursue. It's such a shame, and pretty crazy because it's never-ending. Ultimately, it stems from moms thinking that they're not enough, feeling guilty about their choices and being unsupported in their lives. We have to find ways to move beyond that.'

Jasmin Jefferies agrees. She will be going back to work in her old office-based job within a month and is currently evaluating how to care for her almost three-month-old. 'I get that people feel strongly about certain things regarding our babies,' she says, 'but polarized opinions create this culture of high-reactivity. We end up disagreeing, and in many cases arguing, over how we choose to raise our children. It turns into this group versus that group, when we're all just trying to do our best. Some moms say that those who put their children in daycare are prioritizing their careers over their children, but I've learned to tune those voices out. I've heard some horror stories about daycare, but I also love my job, and as a single mom, I need to work. So I'm doing my research and we'll see how it all feels when I get to that stage. Meanwhile, I just try to mind my own business, do what's best for my daughter and me, and let other parents do the same.'

Wise words to live by. Here are a couple more perspectives that will hopefully ease your guilt, soothe any insecurities and remind you that we're all on the same side, just trying to do the best we can for our children and ourselves. It's a uniquely tough gig, being a mum to a human baby, remember, especially without our fully functioning village on hand. Let's look for ways to support, applaud, mentor and appreciate each other. Whatever our job status.

'I never thought I would want to be a stay-at-home mom. Before I had my daughter, I didn't see myself ever giving less than 100 per cent to my job. While I still find it essential for my wellbeing to work outside the home, I now work part-time, a couple of days a week.'

— Chelsea, US

'I was a stay-at-home mom for two years, but I began to feel that my whole personality was wrapped around my son and I was losing myself. I finally plucked up the courage to look for a job. Those first three weeks of work were hard. I bawled my eyes out every time I had to leave him with his babysitter. But I am very glad I did. I set limits on work so I can make time for my family, but I've also returned to the part of me that likes being independent and in charge!'

— Daisy V.-V., US

Being a mother is not straightforward, whatever your work status and irrespective of whether or not you're paying somebody else to look after your children. You will be mothering and potentially also working for decades to come, so it makes sense that your approach will change with the years. Maybe you'll opt for a gradual return to employment, via part-time hours or switches between sectors. Women tell us about leaving physically demanding jobs in retail for office-based positions, fitness careers for teaching, and becoming self-employed or entrepreneurs, working from home and on their own terms. Other women power back to big jobs in marketing, finance or the law and find that being a mother is a spur to their ambitions. Motherhood can be highly motivating, especially if we want to be a role model for our children. It can give us a dose of clarity about what we're capable of and boost our confidence in our own value. Surely it doesn't matter whether that confidence and clarity steer us towards the workplace, staying at home with the kids, starting our own business, going back to school or taking part in activism or voluntary work, so long as we're following our own path and cheering other women on theirs.

If you're currently at the stage of wondering how to leave your baby or whether you should or could stay at home, please know that although the decisions might feel agonizingly black and white right now, you can and will make them to the best of your ability. You will join the millions of women who have figured out how to mother their kids *and* work, in whatever way is meaningful for them. It's tough but you've got this.

In a nutshell . . .

Feeling anxious, anguished, resentful and guilty over decisions around caring for our kids is common, but there are ways to manage these feelings. It takes practice and thinking hard about where they come from. What are our core beliefs around a mother's obligations? What do we want for ourselves? Our family? What are we ambivalent about? How can we resist the ideology of the perfect mother, treat ourselves and others with compassion and take our own needs a little more seriously?

Decisions about how and when to work outside the home can feel crucial because they touch on our children's welfare and our sense of self. When they come up for discussion, it's easy to feel judged. When that happens, we can become 'judgey' in turn. Rather than letting our insecurities run riot, it might help to channel Jasmin Jefferies: take a deep breath and remember that our decisions are nobody's business but our own. And that goes both ways.

Your value is not defined by your job or your parenting choices. There are as many ways to work, both inside and outside the home, as there are mums with creativity, energy, ideas and determination. Trust that you'll find your way.

CHAPTER 11

Sex, intimacy and invisible labour

On being parents as well as life partners

Your relationship with your partner, if you have one, and especially if they're also the parent of your child, is likely to be taking a bit of a battering right now. Being a mother to an infant is not exactly easily compatible with being romantic, sexual, tender, spontaneous, witty or endlessly patient with your other half's work stresses and housework fails. As a couple, shifting from being just the two of you to a family unit is a huge deal. And you're both tired. No wonder arguments flare up and resentments build. If you're worried about this aspect of your motherhood journey, you're not alone. It's tough.

Itzel Cabrera is 26 and lives in Tulsa, Oklahoma, with her husband and Mateo, their 15-month-old son. Itzel's husband has served in the military and was deployed to Syria when Mateo was two months old, returning just before his first birthday. Itzel is open about the challenges of reconnecting with her partner as a parent and a wife, after nine tough months away from him.

'Obviously we were overjoyed when he came home but it wasn't easy for any of us. We had to figure out how to parent together but also how to reconnect as a couple. I needed to learn how to be a wife again and get back to loving my body and myself, having been through a lot of turmoil about losing my identity after Mateo was born. It was a bit scary to think, *What if he's not patient enough with the baby? What if he's not patient enough with me? What if he has different expectations now? What if this, what if that? Will it hurt the first time we make love?*

'I talked with other moms who had already been through this stage of figuring out how to be parents as well as partners. I asked so many questions. And then I was like, *Okay, I just need to wait.* And oh my gosh, it was just like meeting him all over again. He knew that intimacy was going to be a bit different and was going to take time. Physically he was in great shape, which made me more self-conscious about my body. He had to come to me and say, "I love you. And you gave me a son. I want to see your body." We really wanted to connect again but the baby wasn't sleeping yet, so it was difficult to get time alone. Then I'd be tired, or he was. Plus, every time Mateo saw me holding my husband's hand, he would have a tantrum. We had months of working on, okay, first we gotta be parents, then of course we gotta be a couple, well now we gotta think of us as individuals. What matters to each of us, and how do we make sure we're still making room for that? It's been a lot but we're getting the hang of it together.'

Itzel's situation was unusual, but every couple who become parents have adjustments to make. The transition to new roles can end up exposing problems that were previously hidden. Even for established couples who communicate well, the pressures of caring for a new baby or child and the sudden lack of time, energy, money and personal space are bound to take a toll.

Jill Zucker was forewarned about the tensions and fights to come by a friend with older children. 'She basically told me,

"The first year is the worst. You're gonna want to divorce your husband." That was actually really helpful when I had a lot of rage and jealousy at the beginning because he could sleep and I couldn't. I kept telling myself, *The first year is the worst. It gets easier after that*. And so far, I haven't got to the point of wanting to divorce him,' she adds, laughing.

Like Itzel, some women speak of their appreciation for their partner and their deepening love. Mums tell us about partnerships that falter initially before growing stronger as the couple adjusts. Others talk about their relationship slowly sinking under the strain. Plenty of women separate from their baby's father during their pregnancy or just after the birth and for some women these experiences are emotionally devastating, though they're not for everyone. Mums also describe coming to terms with separation and forming constructive co-parenting relationships with their exes.

Many, many women tell us about relationships that sometimes disappoint them or drive them crazy that they nevertheless value and nurture. Mums keep the faith with their partners through exhausted date nights, awkward attempts to find alone-time for sex, endless squabbles about who's most tired and Cold-War-level stand-offs over whose turn it is to change a nappy.

If you're in a partnership with the parent of your child, you will almost certainly be coming up against issues around how to parent together, how to support one another and how to keep nurturing your relationship. If you're currently struggling, listen up for more words of comfort on everything from nerves around postpartum sex to handling the end of a relationship with as much grace as possible.

From first sex postpartum to rebuilding intimacy for the long term

Being sexually intimate again after you've had a baby can feel . . . *awkward*. Or 'like a chore' or 'not a priority' for touched-out and exhausted mums. Women gave us a lot of short or one-word answers in response to our enquiry about how it was to return to sex postpartum, and although a few people told us it was 'amazing', more said it was 'painful' and 'scary'.

The impact of birth injuries was a subject that came up a lot, with some women reporting that pain and serious discomfort was still an issue up to a year after giving birth. If this is the case for you, take heart from Roslynn W.'s experience. 'I had some challenges with my pelvic floor that made intercourse painful but after seeing a perinatal chiropractor and doing therapy, I enjoy intercourse more than ever.' Lots of women mentioned their gratitude to the doctors who took them seriously and referred them to therapists or prescribed medication. Sex can and does return to being pleasurable and positive. Sometimes it just takes time and patience, as Yvonne E. from the US explained. 'Sex was painful for me at first, but once I got through that, the intimacy and pleasure from being sexually active helped us reconnect and adjust to our new life together.'

Even if sex isn't painful for you, there are plenty of other obstacles to a happy sex life post-kids. The hormonal changes associated with breastfeeding are known to lower libido, being exhausted is a total passion-killer and opportunities are not exactly plentiful, especially if your child sleeps in your room. It's hardly surprising if sex happens 'much less often and is much less adventurous than it was before'. For some women it feels like just another thing on the to-do list. Kerry from the UK told us, 'Honestly, I just can't be bothered.'

Mama, we hear you. If you've spent all day breastfeeding and cuddling your child, you might be longing for some personal space rather than having yet another person's body in your zone. 'While I was breastfeeding, there was absolutely NOTHING sexy about my boobs being touched by my partner,' Elizabeth K. from the US told us. 'I would feel guilty about not wanting to be intimate and then try and force myself to do it, which hurt my mental health.'

Guilt and resentment . . . that all too familiar toxic combination that can leave us feeling down on ourselves and our partner. Peanut Professional Heather Shannon is a US-based certified sex therapist, and host of the *Ask a Sex Therapist* podcast. She sees these difficult emotions all the time with her clients. 'A mum is touched out, the kids have been grabbing at them, they're breastfeeding, they haven't had a moment to themselves. I suggest that the parent who's been out all day spends an hour with the kids, while the primary caregiver goes off and spends time alone, not doing chores, just relaxing and getting into the mood for intimacy.' Heather stresses that this doesn't need to be intercourse and that foreplay is as much about 'relaxation, flirting and compliments' as anything physical.

Maintaining a satisfying sexual relationship can feel daunting when you're tired and still adjusting to the new role of parent. It's not easy to figure out how that sits alongside being a partner and lover. Heather has some refreshingly no-nonsense suggestions. 'Don't wait for the kids to be asleep,' she says, 'because that can end up being too late when you're already exhausted. Look for opportunities throughout the day to connect physically. These can be simple little touches like a kiss on the cheek, holding hands while walking the dog or a hand on the knee while watching TV.'

It helps to be as kind as possible, with ourselves and each other, as we adjust to a phase of life that inevitably comes with a lot of constraints. Life as a couple will be different for a while, but it can still be rich and rewarding. 'Take it easy on yourself and each other,' Heather says.

Sex often slips down your priority list in early motherhood, but it can bring so many benefits for your personal wellbeing as well as your relationship. Women talk about sex becoming more meaningful after having children, despite struggling with a loss of confidence in their body's appearance and constant exhaustion. The deeper emotional connection with their partner, having been through the life-changing impact of parenthood together, can be a powerful boost to intimacy.

Self-consciousness comes up over and over again. 'I really didn't like my body for a long, long, long time,' Becca A. told us. 'I lived in baggy clothes. I didn't want my husband to touch me. I got to the point where I had to explain to him that I needed his help to feel confident. I needed to hear him say, "You look fantastic, your body looks amazing." And he's not the greatest with words, so that wasn't an easy thing for either of us. Wanting to have sex again has been one of many things that took me way longer than I expected. But we're getting there now, which is good because I could feel that we were more distant if we weren't intimate.' Becca and her husband figured it out by being vulnerable together, communicating honestly about what they needed and being generous with each other. It was a little awkward, but patience and communication pulled them through.

One other, very fundamental block to physical intimacy and the emotional intimacy it relies on is finding any alone time with your partner. Heather insists that prioritizing this is crucial. 'If you never have any time away from the children your relationship becomes nothing but co-parenting, and that can lead to the end of some partnerships. You need to go on dates occasionally, which means you need childcare. If cost is a worry, you could find another family to swap with – they watch your kids, then you watch theirs. Prioritize time for just the two of you, to have a cuddle, talk about something else, get out of the house, or have sex.'

The washing-up battles – conflicts and disappointments

It's no surprise that rows over money and housework often peak when you become parents. If you used to split the chores 50/50, you might find that's no longer possible when your whole routine has to shift around. Old compromises don't necessarily work any more. Maybe you previously overlooked the washing-up in the sink or the dirty clothes on the bathroom floor because your partner was a great cook and always took the bins out. But now that you're both exhausted, your partner doesn't cook as much and they still aren't doing the damn washing-up.

Financial contributions and money management may have been blown wide open by maternity leave and the cost of setting up for a baby. It can be a nasty shock to realize that you're financially dependent on your partner, especially when the bills are mounting up.

When work, money and new roles intersect, the strain can

cause more arguments. Many women tell us that they and their partner are having a hard time feeling like equal members of the same team. It's common to end up fighting over who does more, or what's harder – being out all day earning a living or being at home all day with a fussy baby and endless household chores.

Many of us feel motherhood has turned us into a domestic drudge. That can lead to everything from mild disappointment to outright fury with our (typically male) partners. Sometimes the issue is a lack of help with the kids. 'My child's father never helps, so I'm the one who's always with our son. I love my little one but it's exhausting to play both roles of parenthood,' as Elba C. from the US puts it. Often, dads are enthusiastic about being with the children but much less so about taking on any of the mundane tasks that family life depends on. Mums are typically quick to acknowledge when their partner is great with the kids, especially in ways that make a big practical difference. As Jill Z. says, 'My husband changed all the diapers for two months when I was breastfeeding on demand. I'll never forget that.' But they also notice when their partner is keen on the fun stuff like playing games and bathtime but not the boring repetitive chores. Not the washing-up.

Veronica Cisneros helps couples find ways through their gripes. She tries to help people see what *they* bring to arguments rather than what their partner brings, because that can unlock ways of doing things differently. On the subject of the washing-up, she has clear advice: 'If you want your partner to wash the dishes, ask them to do it and then . . . *let them do it.* Even if that means waiting two days for it to happen. Don't get frustrated that they didn't do it before you went to bed, take over the task yourself and then lash out at them in the morning – that approach isn't effective. Let them do it. Nine times out of ten, those dishes will get done – maybe not on your timetable but eventually. Your partner will have learned something rather than being the failure again. You will have learned something too.'

I wish he would just help me with chores rather than me having to write him a damn list every week! My advice would be to sit down much sooner than we did and talk about who's doing what. We ended up taking out our frustrations on each other.

— Gajski K., UK

On top of the old classics of sex, money and housework, you now have a new topic to fall out over: how to bring up the kids. A lot of women only discover after they have them that their views on how to bring up children are very different from their partner or co-parent's. Mums often tell us they're following gentle parenting, but their partner favours more discipline, or that they're keen on a hands-off Montessori-style approach while their partner is more of a helicopter parent. 'My husband is generally very supportive and spends a lot of time with the kids so I can have a break,' said Julia O. from the UK. 'But we never talked about what parenting means to us before having kids, and our parenting styles are different so sometimes it's hard to relate to one another.' Kara B. from the US said she and her husband 'butt heads all the time on parenting styles. I think he's much harder on our son than he ever was on our girls and I don't agree with it!' We all bring a set of assumptions as well as intentions to our parenting style, and it can be hard to find the healthy, productive way to communicate about issues that feel so important to get right.

Even if you're in alignment with your partner or co-parent on the big stuff, different approaches day to day can trigger resentment, as Katarina A. from the US told us. 'My husband and I have disagreements on screen time, chores and snacks but the biggest issue is that he doesn't always stick to what I've established as a stay-at-home mom. I believe consistency makes things easier over time. When he disrupts that in favour of what's easier in the moment, I feel frustrated if that causes an issue later. For example, my husband will put on TV for the kids first thing in the morning. But I've found that if they don't use their brains and move their bodies early in the day, the younger two won't nap, and then they're going to be an extra handful.'

As well as resentment there can be a lot of sadness when we feel distance or blame creeping in, rather than the appreciation and affection we're longing for. Many of us dream of help being freely offered, of more attention, companionship and love. 'I really miss him,' one UK-based mum told us, sadly. And then there's the deadly poison of contempt. Veronica is adamant that contempt is a killer of relationships like nothing else. It's hard to forget or to forgive if we sense that our partner is treating us with this cold and superior brand of loathing. Hopefully you're not having to contend with it, but be vigilant because it can creep in. Making statements such as 'I am a good mother because I connect with our child and you are a terrible father because you never do,' for example, is highly contemptuous. The antidote is vulnerability. And kindness.

There was a point when I thought my partner no longer loved me and was only sticking around because of the baby. When I finally got the courage to ask him about

*this, he didn't say I was being stupid or crazy. He just
said, 'Of course I love you.' Being vulnerable with him
made my worries much less intense and showed him
that he could be vulnerable too.*

— **Helen M., UK**

Partners turned parents – new identities for both of you

So what's the answer? What helps with the resentment, or
the sadness that your romance has shrivelled into wrangling
over the logistics of family life? There's no magic wand – but
you wouldn't expect that, right? There's only patience, vulnerability, kindness and talking it over. Above all, there's trust
that it will get better in time. Because when your day to day
is exhausting and your partnership can't be your top priority
any more, sometimes all you can do is hang in there until you
get a little breathing space. Try to remember that both of you
are going through big changes as individuals, as is your relationship. Just as some women find motherhood relatively easy
to incorporate into their identity while others struggle profoundly, some couples flow gracefully between being partners
and parents, but many – probably most – do not.

Here's Thea from the UK, expressing the frustrations that
so many of us feel as we're navigating this new territory. 'Our
baby is four months old and we haven't been intimate since
he was born. I feel like we are just housemates. We lose our
temper with each other a lot more easily. Sometimes I feel like
it's my responsibility to teach him how to parent, when I'm
learning how to do it as I go along. It's taken me by surprise
as we always used to agree.'

Thea says she's worried that things won't get easier and that she and her husband are somehow failing. We can reassure her and every single one of you mamas who might be feeling the same that, actually, she and her husband are doing just fine. Despite the tense words and the lack of sex and the grumbles over him going out with mates when she's stuck at home breastfeeding. *Their baby is only four months old.* Remember Jill's mantra from the beginning of this chapter? 'The first year is the worst. You're gonna want to divorce your husband.' Or recall Itzel and her husband's wisdom, when they said they wanted to help each other be parents, partners and also *themselves.* Keep looking for ways to talk, be vulnerable, make each other laugh, have a cuddle and remember what you like about each other. Give yourselves grace and keep looking for connection, to each other and yourselves.

> *Between the different parenting styles, the roommate stage and the lack of sleep there has definitely been an increase in arguments and resentment. Our communication has improved, though. We talk about what's going right and wrong now and we are working to get back to our husband-and-wife roles.*
>
> **— Valerie C., US**

Heather joins the dots between intimacy, wellbeing and identity for her clients, reminding people that 'sex, intimacy, mental health and physical health are all so connected, though we rarely treat them that way. If you're dealing with post-partum depression, for example, your libido is likely to be low. Sexual energy is life-force energy, and depression is a dimming of the life-force. What can you do to nourish and nurture that inner spark?'

Heather says that although communication skills are definitely key to rebuilding intimacy and a secure and happy partnership, you need to know what you want in order to be able to communicate it. 'Your identity shifts so much when you become a parent. What are you missing about being a human rather than a mom or a wife? Maybe it's seeing your friends without your partner and kid, going to the gym, or playing the piano. How can you make time for that? It will take a little more planning than it used to, but it's worth making space for that thing that's going to make you feel like you. One of the many benefits is that you can then start to rebuild connection with your partner from a solid foundation.'

During the good times I adore him more than ever. Other times I despise him. But if you don't communicate what you expect and want from a partner, you will (sometimes) be disappointed. I wish I had communicated what I needed from him sooner.

— Kelston R., Australia

There is still plenty of adoration among the parenting life partners in our community. Mums tell us about falling in love all over again as they watch their partner bonding with their baby and striving to be a great father. It's good to recognize and celebrate the wonderful partners and the couples who are finding their way. It's also good to recognize that not every couple will make it, and that doesn't have to be a disaster. Plenty of parent-partners split up, that's the reality; but they can still be effective co-parents and honour themselves as they part ways.

Sarah Vincent is 29 and lives in Hampshire in the UK. She has a seven-month-old son. His father left the relationship just after she found out she was pregnant. 'We'd been together for seven years,' she says, 'and had talked about having kids at some point but the pregnancy was a surprise, and he just freaked out completely. It was really hard managing my feelings and I did feel lonely, but he is a good dad. He came to the birth and is very involved with our son and supports me to have my own life. We're on good terms 90 per cent of the time now. We're in what I would describe as a really healthy co-parenting relationship.'

There are many ways to have a successful relationship, as Sarah's gracious, pragmatic attitude demonstrates. Whether you're still feeling the love with your life partner or are realizing that you need to leave them, whether you're on day one of that difficult first year or day 365 of a slightly easier second year, we salute you for finding and following your own best path through this complex terrain.

In a nutshell . . .

Time without your kids is the first step to rebuilding intimacy. That means finding childcare, whether by paying a sitter or making an arrangement with a friend or family member. That might feel like a cost you can't afford or a hassle you can't face, but if you want your partnership to make it back out of the roommate stage, it's vital.

Open communication is more important than ever. You might never have faced challenges like this as a couple, or coped with such a huge personal transition. Everything about your current life will be increasing the pressure and making you feel vulnerable. That's a risk to your relationship but also an opportunity. If you can find ways to communicate, you can grow together, enjoy this unique time and come through stronger.

Contempt is a silent killer of relationships. Do whatever you can to avoid it. It can't take hold when you work through your resentments. And aim to be open, vulnerable and kind. At least more often than not. You're only human, after all.

PART FOUR
Reaching a year

CHAPTER 12

Will this baby ever sleep?

On exhaustion, frustration and learning to trust

When we asked our community what they missed from their life pre-kids, only freedom was mentioned more frequently than sleep. Of parents to infants under one, it's close to 75 per cent who said they were craving a full night of uninterrupted, restorative, blissful, glorious sleep.

Sleep deprivation is the absolute pits, as any parent of a baby or toddler will tell you. It can feel hard to fathom how something as basic as clocking up at least five measly consecutive hours of uninterrupted sleep can turn into the Holy Grail, a prize worth more than rubies, and the object of deep envy directed at everyone in the world who's sleeping through the night. Couples with non-sleeping kids get into toxic games of competitive tiredness. Single parents turn into zombies. Sleep deprivation, unlike mere tiredness, is a silent killer of wellbeing, joy and purpose. It hollows you out and makes every other stress and strain infinitely harder. Unfortunately, it's also virtually certain to be part of your life for anywhere between three months (for a few lucky parents) and three years (our commiserations).

'You won't die of tiredness,' one exhausted mum reported being told by a brisk nurse at her child's six-month check-up.

Maybe not – as long as you don't nod off while driving – but extreme tiredness definitely is a threat to your physical, mental and emotional health. Not to scare you (because who wants scare tactics?) but prolonged poor sleep has been linked with PND and postpartum anxiety as well as cognitive impairment and cardiovascular strain. It's a big deal, and if your child is still waking every other hour as you head into the second half of their first year, you can be forgiven for feeling despair nibbling at your mind.

Will this baby ever sleep? is a simple question with a simple answer – yes, they will. At some point. But when, and how? And what can you do to speed up that glorious moment when they sleep for four, five or even six hours in a row, reliably, so that you can stop feeling like a total wreck?

Honest answer: we have no idea. And in any case, you've probably already tried every tip you've ever dredged up from a forum at four in the morning. All we can do to ease your pain is share other mums' pain. You are not alone. Oh, and remind you that, somehow, you will survive. Perhaps the single most useful thing you can do is trust in that. As Mitra from London said, 'When my first child was about three months old and wasn't sleeping, a friend with older children said to me, "Oh, don't worry, in another six or seven months they'll be sleeping through the night." And I was like, *what*? I cannot do this for another six or seven months. But, of course, I did. I've just had my second baby and although I'm dreading the tiredness, I'm not anxious about it. I know from experience that it's difficult, but it will come to an end.'

Baby sleep – the ultimate problem with no solution?

Co-sleeping, nap schedules, sleep training, consistent bedtime routines, gradual withdrawal of parental presence, swaddling, weighted blankets, white-noise machines, keep the room cool, top up with formula at last feed of the day, feed on demand round the clock, don't let them fall asleep on the breast, make sure you teach them to self-soothe, give them every comfort they require, use a dummy, a snuggly, never ever let them suck their thumb . . .

The list of advice, tips, tools and general info overload around infant sleeping can be enough to bring on insomnia. If your baby or toddler doesn't sleep for long, or only sleeps when you're holding them, or both, then your child sleeping through the night in their own bassinet or bed can become an obsession. And where there are desperate obsessed parents, there are experts offering solutions. There's a whole industry of sleep consultants who promise to arrive in your home with their clever techniques and professional experience and solve the problem. For some parents, these consultants are immensely helpful; for others, not so much.

It's almost as if the problem of how to get your child to sleep for longer stretches of time, preferably at night and without you, is a classic example of *the baby-related problem with no solution*. A baby needs to eat little and often – and there's no way round that. Some children are extra fretful, they have particular needs – and there's no way round that. And then, if your child has never slept through the night and they're now a toddler, it's learned behaviour – and unlearning it is pretty tricky. Whatever the causes, you end up with a problem with no solution. Or rather, a problem that nine times out of ten eventually resolves itself, either because something you try helps or enough time passes and the child just . . . *figures it out*. Like we said, we're not experts, but we do know that worrying about how to fix this, while natural, can make everything feel even harder.

> When you're up at 4 a.m. trying to work out how to get
> your baby to sleep, online mums' communities can be
> invaluable. You might get tips (white noise really helped
> us, for example) but even if the tips don't work, the
> sense that other people are going through the same
> thing is so comforting. It stops you from feeling like a
> failure, or that you're going mad.
>
> — Dr Zoya, UK

Kylie, who lives in California, gets wild-eyed when she talks about (lack of) sleep – her son's and her own. 'He's 20 months old now and has never been a sleeper. He slept on my chest for the first eight months of his life. Oh god, it was awful. Thank goodness I don't move in my sleep, I would just lie like I was in a coffin, in a recliner with him on my chest. It drove me crazy. I would be on a chat group and people would be saying, "Oh, my kids slept through the night since they were four months old." I'm like, how? *How?* My son went through a few weeks where he was sleeping ten-hour stretches. I thought we'd mastered it. And then he stopped. We ended up paying $1,000 for a sleep expert to come to our house. Oh, all the stuff. I think having a supportive partner who shares the load with me is absolutely the reason I haven't just fallen over the edge. It's getting better now, but slowly, and I don't feel I can trust it yet because, as I say, we've had improvements and regressions.'

Sleep regression – two words to strike fear into any mama's heart. A regression is what happens when a child's sleeping pattern suddenly changes for the worse. Maybe they can no longer settle themselves at bedtime, or they go back to waking up several times a night. Regressions triggered by growth spurts and development milestones often occur at four months, between eight and ten months, and around a year, but they can also be related to teething or an illness. They usually only last two to four weeks – but those weeks can feel loooong.

Marcia's daughter is only four and a half months old so it's early days, but the family has just gone through a sleep regression and Marcia, self-described sleep-lover, is reeling. 'At around three months the baby started sleeping five hours at night and we were ecstatic. And then this week, it's just been awful. All my toughest moments since becoming a mother have been connected to my exhaustion. One night recently I came upstairs, woke my wife and I was like, "I'm sorry but I cannot do this." I handed the baby over and I sat there and cried. I hate to say it, but all those videos they make you watch at antenatal classes about "don't shake your baby" . . . we were like, *Oh, what a fucking joke. We would never shake our baby.* And of course I never would, but until you've been there you can't really grasp the combination of helplessness, frustration and exhaustion. I understand why they show those videos now. You have to get on with caring for your child, despite your exhaustion. And I did, once I'd had a little cry.'

Lack of sleep makes everything else harder

Sleep deprivation and poor mental health go hand in hand. Taylor Murray, whose story about acute postpartum anxiety we heard earlier in the book, says that her difficulties had been building throughout her pregnancy, but it was the first month of sleep deprivation that tipped her into crisis. Many mums report severe emotional disruption brought on by exhaustion, which can hit early or build up over many months.

It can be scary to acknowledge that disturbed sleep is affecting you more than you expected. It might feel like a badge of failure, or make you feel ashamed that you can't cope with something that everyone has to go through. After all, it's not exactly news that parents of infants are tired, right? If this is you, please cut yourself some slack. Unless you've done night shifts or suffered from severe insomnia, you've probably never encountered sleep deprivation on this scale before. As we said and you know, it's not just feeling extra tired. It's much more debilitating than that. So if you're not feeling well and you suspect that lack of sleep is becoming unbearable, please ask for help.

Amy Thomas from Nottingham was already dealing with a lot when her daughter went through a sleep regression that almost tipped her over the edge. She was a young single parent, having chosen to split up from her baby's father in the days after the birth when he revealed himself to be controlling and indifferent to her welfare. Amy's mum and siblings stepped in to help, but the strain of dealing with her ex-partner made everything else feel even harder.

'My family were brilliant, but they were working and I was doing all the night times so I was exhausted. I had postnatal depression. I was getting to the point where I thought, if I don't focus on myself right now, I'm not gonna be here.' We'll be coming back to Amy's story and the emotional ins and outs of sleep training and controlled crying later in the chapter.

Meanwhile it's worth noting that while exhaustion *can* lead to serious problems, it doesn't always; even when mums have dealt with significant anxiety or depression previously. Grace Williams, who struggled with PND in the first three months of her son's life, told us that he still wasn't sleeping consistently as he neared his first birthday, but she was coping okay. 'The other night I had an eight-hour hit out of him but for the most part, for the last 11 months I've had two hours' sleep at a time. We're going to be back in the trenches when I return to work next week.' Despite being a little nervous about working while sleep-deprived, Grace said she didn't feel the tiredness was putting her mental health back at risk. Overall, she was feeling better prepared for difficulties now than she did immediately after giving birth. Proof that even after a rocky start to motherhood, sleep deprivation won't necessarily feel intolerable.

Aside from mental health, being exhausted also impacts relationships with our nearest and dearest, from life partners to other children. Jill Z. acknowledged this, saying, 'Our baby is ten months old now and if you put him in our bed, he'll sleep all night. Put him in his cot, and he's just not into it. I think my husband is feeling the lack of intimacy worse than I am. I'm still so tired, so that's all I care about. I come back to this belief that our son will sleep more as he gets older. My husband and I will find time to be just the two of us together.' As well as the impact on intimacy, you might find yourself disagreeing with your partner over how to tackle the issue itself. Lots of mums tell us they end up in ongoing rows over sleep training, controlled crying or whether to invest in a sleep consultant.

When you have a second or subsequent child, of course, even if you've managed to get the older one settled into reliable sleeping, your new arrival has a long way to go. If the gap between your children is small, that can add up to years of accumulated sleep deprivation, not to mention possible regression from your older kid. Kat W., who has two under two, is currently dealing with exactly this. 'Teddy was really good at sleeping in his own room, but as soon as Florence appeared, Teddy was bad at sleeping in his own room. He wanted to come back into our bed. I'm just taking the path of least resistance at this stage.' Fair enough!

I didn't appreciate the advice from health visitors. They suggested very basic things that of course we had tried and that hadn't worked. In the end we told them he was sleeping better even when he wasn't, so that we could avoid the unhelpful advice. And we went with the flow and somehow got through it.

— Hannah B., UK

Surviving long-term exhaustion

For many children, between six months and a year marks the point at which they start to sleep for longer stretches. The experts will tell you that this is tied to developmental issues in the brain and digestive system. Things settle down, basically, and the exact timetable varies from child to child. It's blissful relief when you gradually realize that there hasn't been a sleep regression lately and things are definitely getting easier. But a year on a severely disrupted sleep schedule, even *six months*, is a tough gig – so if you're just getting through it, congratulations, we're pleased for you.

What if things still aren't getting better? Some children struggle to sleep through the night for years. This can undermine the whole family's wellbeing, prevent people from having more children and drive a wedge between couples. It can also turn into an existential problem with no solution, especially if there doesn't seem to be any reason for it.

First things first: sometimes ongoing sleep difficulties can be down to health issues or complex emotional needs. If you feel you've tried everything and nothing helps, if you're worried about your child and feeling unwell yourself from exhaustion, don't delay. Go to see your doctor. You might be worried you'll be fobbed off because 'babies don't sleep and being tired won't kill you'. If that happens (and it might), please try again. You and your child deserve it. There are charities that support children with extra needs who have sleep issues, such as Scope in the UK or The Sleep Foundation in the US. They have a range of resources, advice and lists of accredited specialists to contact.

And if you're chronically sleepless as you're coming towards or already past your child's first birthday, we want to give you a huge hug and a bouquet of flowers. Coping with worry related to your child's wellbeing is hard enough. If you're also dealing with your own long-term exhaustion, it's a heroic slog.

Claudia Tomalino's 15-month-old daughter still wakes up every two or three hours through the night and it's still mostly on Claudia to go to her. 'I'm so tired I just go to the default mode, which is breastfeeding. If I don't, it's screaming for hours. I know it's not fair on her because I start to resent her as well as my partner. I have to change. I just don't know how.'

Claudia is beginning to wonder whether her daughter might have additional needs. 'I read online about high-needs children and though I'm not yet sure that describes my daughter, I could relate. It was a relief to know that there are other mums feeling the way I do. It made me feel less like a failure and less guilty about being envious of parents who moan about being woken once a night. I feel terrible about these feelings, but being this tired is the most difficult thing I've ever done and I just feel primitively jealous of anyone who's sleeping.'

Claudia resents her partner while admitting that they've *both* got into a situation in which the only thing that soothes their daughter back to sleep is breastfeeding. It's a common predicament. If you have a live-in partner with whom you *can* take turns, that's great, though how you figure out the tag-teaming might also be a source of tension, given that you're probably both exhausted by now. It will take some open, honest, generous and non-accusatory communication. Dr Zoya and her husband agreed that if either one of them was really struggling, they could raise it with the other. 'We'd do this thing where I'd say, I've only got 45 per cent left to give. He'd say, okay, I've got 48 per cent so I'll do the night shift tonight.' If you have a spare room, or any space that's far enough away from the baby so that you won't hear them, you might take it in turns to sleep there. Try not to get into big fights over who is most tired. Look for practical and emotional ways to help each other.

That's our cue for another sticky topic . . . sleep training. Is it okay to sleep train your child? If so, when and how? Are there better and worse ways to do it? Can controlled crying ever be okay? And should you try a baby sleep consultant?

The Sticky Stuff:
Sleep training and baby sleep consultants

Claudia says she feels guilty, resentful, judged and judgemental about how her daughter sleeps compared to other children. Sleeping, like feeding, is one of those issues that's emotional dynamite among parents. And when it comes to sleep training – by which we mean a range of structured methods for getting your child into the habit of settling themselves at night and sleeping for longer without you – people have opinions and are not shy to tell you about them.

The elements of sleep training that really provoke strong views centre on allowing your child to cry without comforting them. There's a spectrum here. Controlled crying, for example, is a process that involves checking on your child but not picking them up, and increasing the length of time you leave it before you go to them. With controlled crying you set a time limit, say 20 or 30 minutes, at which point you do go and comfort your child. It's different from the 'cry it out' method, when having followed a care-and-comfort routine and checked on their safety, you then leave your child to cry themselves to sleep. Some parents and experts claim, on the one hand, that this is tantamount to child abuse, while others say it was all over in 48 hours and they wish they'd done it earlier. Plenty of people will tell you that controlled crying was tough but has saved their family from implosion.

As ever, we're not going to debate the merits of the issue, just acknowledge how difficult it is for mums to agonize over. The problem feels enormous, the stakes are high and we're so damn tired that (obviously) we can't think straight. Asking for advice or even just talking about it with other mums can feel frightening and shameful. Claudia said, 'One friend who had older kids was choosing a very different approach from mine. She put her babies in their own room very early. I can take this advice, maybe think about it, but I'm not ready to implement it. I've mostly stopped talking to friends because I feel I'm moaning about something I should be able to change. So I just do more research . . . I'm stuck.'

Kylie H. recognizes the sense of failure that Claudia describes. 'I started to think, am I just bad at this? How come I can't help my child to fall and stay asleep, which is a very basic thing? It made me feel so inadequate.' Kylie also relates to the desperate search for answers, and the comparing what's worked for others with what hasn't yet worked for us. 'When our son was about six months old, we tried this programme called Taking Care of Babies, which was recommended by friends. I would *see* it working for them. It took them just five minutes to put their child down for a nap. But it was hell for us. Going in and checking on our son every 15 minutes made everything worse. He would see us, feel a little bit of relief, and then we'd walk out of the room again. There would be two hours of crying and distress for everyone. At his nine-month appointment, we told our paediatrician he was still sleeping on us for all sleeps. He was like, "You guys are doing something wrong."' At this point Kylie says with a grin, 'I think it's important to note that my paediatrician is a lovely doctor who doesn't have children. Anyway, he referred us to a sleep consultant.'

That experience was a mixed bag. Kylie admits that she was hoping for a magic bullet and didn't get it, but the consultant did make some useful observations. 'She pointed out that we needed a calmer, more minimalist routine with less talking. And she said that nursing him to sleep every time really needed tackling. She encouraged me to experiment with taking him off the boob so he could fall asleep in my arms.'

The most helpful thing for Kylie was that the consultant presented all this as a process of trial and error, which would take time. 'Eventually we figured out, for example, that making breastfeeding the first element in the routine rather than the last meant he could learn that boob wasn't the signal to sleep. I would feed him, then my husband would step in and change his diaper, put his pyjamas on, read him a couple of books and then put him in the sleep sack and into the crib.'

What about controlled crying?

There are few more divisive issues than controlled crying, and especially 'cry it out'. But if it does work for you, then you and your baby might be sleeping through the night within days, with all the benefits for everyone's wellbeing that come along with a happy and relaxed parent and child.

Amy Thomas had exactly this experience. On her return from a desperately needed two nights away from Anna, her five-month-old daughter, she discovered that her mum had started to get Anna into a routine, something that had always been really difficult for Amy to manage as a single parent with PND. 'I had been co-sleeping and breastfeeding on demand through the night, so I didn't know when Anna was waking or when she was full,' Amy explains. 'There was no routine at all. My milk supply started to fail because I was so stressed and ill, which meant Anna wasn't getting enough, and we both went from loving breastfeeding to finding it difficult and sad. I was so exhausted that I was almost delirious. I fell asleep one day when Anna was napping on me, and when I woke I saw she'd slipped off my chest, which really scared me. We were in bed and she was absolutely fine but I panicked that if I was this exhausted, I couldn't guarantee to keep her safe. I felt I was letting my daughter down in every way. My family urged me to go away so I could sleep for two consecutive nights. We agreed that my mum would get up with Anna and give her formula from a bottle. I had been dead set on exclusive breastfeeding until she was at least six months, so this really upset me, but Anna was happy to take a bottle and I felt like I had to try something different. When I got back, my mum had managed to establish the basics of a night-time routine. That night I followed it at 7 p.m., and Anna went straight to sleep. I sat and cried with relief.'

Amy's mother helped her to continue with sleep training over the next two weeks, and though it was tough at times, within a fortnight Anna was sleeping for up to eight hours a night. Amy followed the same consistent steps every time. Anna would have a bath, listen to the same lullabies, have a bottle, then go in her sleep bag. By the time she was eight months old, she was consistently sleeping eight hours a night straight through. But the controlled crying, and especially the 'cry it out' elements, were tough.

'Sleep training wasn't easy,' says Amy. 'I had to sit in the garden and watch the camera on the baby monitor with the sound turned down so I couldn't hear her crying. It broke my heart. As a mum, you just want to solve everything. You want the tears to stop. I hated the thought that she might be feeling abandoned or that she was crying herself to sleep. But I knew that in the long term it was going to benefit her and it was going to benefit me. Mum was a huge help. If it got too distressing for me or for Anna, she would go to her and then reassure me that the process was working and that I wasn't being a terrible mother; I was actually doing something positive for my child.

'I honestly believe that using a combination of controlled crying and cry it out saved me and my family. If I'd stayed that tired and my PND had got worse, I don't know what would have happened. It enabled me to be the best possible mother to my daughter.

I know it doesn't work for all babies or all families and I don't think I could have done it for month after month, but we didn't have to because it was relatively straightforward and we began to see improvements within days. You couldn't take it on without another adult to back you up, though. I could not have done it without the hands-on support and emotional reassurance from my own mum.'

Kylie has a different take. She was uncomfortable with the sleep consultant's suggestion to incorporate controlled crying into training. 'She advised letting him cry for up to 25 minutes, which I found incredibly difficult. We did try it, but it wasn't a magic fix for us as it is for some people. Even three months later he was still crying for nearly half an hour before finally falling asleep. It never sat well with me, but I kept trying until he turned one, and then I just thought, that's enough. I had begun to feel more confident in myself by then. I could see that for my son, and for us, none of these techniques were going to provide a fix. He just didn't want to sleep as early in the evening or for as long as other babies, and he needed much more help to get to sleep than some others. I started to think that was okay, and I guess because there were some small improvements, and I had a lot of help from my partner, I felt less stressed and less like I was failing. I went back to being with him as he was settling. Even now that he's coming up for two, I still lie down next to him and just hold his hand as he's falling asleep. And I think that's fine. It doesn't take long these days, and I enjoy it.'

We're all different

Every baby (and in fact every human being) has different sleep needs. 'I'm a higher-sleep-need person than my husband,' says Kylie. 'I think my son is just much more like his father, but it took me a while to get to know that about him. I was constantly comparing him to other babies when maybe I needed to accept he was himself — low sleep needs and all.'

Amy and Kylie's stories show us something crucial: that no two babies are going to respond in the same way to the same situation. While asking for advice and suggestions from other parents and experts is a great idea, we're not obliged to take them, and we *really* don't need to beat ourselves up if they don't work for us and our baby. If the advice is making us feel worse, then it's fair enough to set it aside. We can always just take what's useful, as Kylie did from her sleep consultant, and leave what's not.

When it comes to controlled crying and sleep training in general, this spirit of trying things out with curiosity rather than desperation, and steering away from making harsh judgements of ourselves or other people, is so important. Because while sleep is crucial, it's not easy and we're all just struggling towards what works for us and the children we love.

Perhaps surviving your baby's disrupted sleep lies in accepting that there is no magical fix for a problem sleeper. No one-size-fits-all solution. Maybe it's not even, or not *exactly*, a problem at all. Kylie says that what's helped her more than anything is reframing the situation. 'I decided to focus on the relationship I was building with my child, rather than thinking of disrupted sleep as a problem to fix. I wish I had given myself more grace in learning who he was and how we were going to work together. I wish I'd had access to wisdom and reassurance from other more experienced moms earlier on. I might have suffered less and enjoyed it more. But we all have to learn this in our own way, because being a mom is unlike any other relationship. The skills you need are not skills you can learn as you did in school or college. That's the challenge, but it's also the joy.'

Both Kylie and Amy stress that coping with sleep issues, however you tackle them, is absolutely not something you can handle on your own for long. Kylie said her partner saved her from going over the edge but also says it could have been 'any loving committed adult who's prepared to stay up at night with you for a week or so, and help you deal with it. That could be your mom or your sibling. I just needed another person with me who was also hearing him cry, also trying to comfort and feed him.' Amy put it very simply when she said that she couldn't have carried out controlled crying without the support of her mum. This makes total sense. Nobody can parent round the clock on their own.

Which brings us to the other thing that really, really helps . . . a night off, so you can go somewhere and *get some sleep*. Even if that means your child having to cope without you, and your partner, mother-in-law or rock-star best friend having to cope with a wailing baby. They will all survive. And the difference it will make to you? Life-changing. The real fix for a problem sleeper is the village it takes to raise a child and their mother. Your village.

In a nutshell . . .

Give yourself permission to make any adjustments to your routine that might help. Prioritize getting your basic needs met as simply as possible. Nap during the day, even if the house is untidy. Eat healthy snacks rather than trying to cook dinner. It's easy to underestimate how long this phase might go on for but also easy to overestimate and catastrophize that it will go on for ever. It won't. Keep the faith.

If you have a partner you can share the load with, try to have open and generous conversations about how you're doing. Look for new baby sleep tips together so that it doesn't become all your problem. Try to find ways to support each other. If you don't have a live-in partner, is there anyone else who can come and do a night shift? Even one night of decent rest can be enough to change your perspective and make you feel human again.

If you have the money, consider bringing in professionals. From postpartum doulas to night nannies to sleep consultants, there are people who might be able to help. Ask around for trusted recommendations, try not to expect miracles and keep an open mind about different approaches.

Or perhaps stop thinking of your child's sleep as a problem to fix. If endless research is increasing your distress, you might find it most helpful simply to stop seeking solutions and switch into a mindset of trusting that you and your family can and will come through this challenge. Standard advice on insomnia is to try to avoid worrying about not sleeping, since that makes everything worse. Same here.

CHAPTER 13

I miss my old body

On body blues and working towards self-acceptance

Becca A. talks with candour about not recognizing the post-partum body she saw in the mirror. Twenty months after her daughter's birth, she still refers to her pre-pregnancy body as her 'normal' body, while also admitting that there is now a new normal. Becca, like many mums, is ambivalent about the physical changes brought about by pregnancy, childbirth and breastfeeding.

'I remember looking at myself in the mirror not long after I'd given birth and thinking, *This is a totally different body from the one I've been looking at for years.* My boobs, my belly, every-thing apart from my hands and feet looked different, even my face. In the last month I've started to feel my body's a bit more familiar to me, but I don't think it's ever going to be exactly as it was. I've been trying to eat healthily and I run around after my daughter a lot, but I haven't had the energy to go back to a proper exercise regime. I did try when she was very little. I went with friends from my prenatal class to the gym. We would all take our babies, put them in the crèche and do a class. I enjoyed it initially and I felt quite motivated to get back in shape. But then I stopped. It was too soon and I was so exhausted. I just thought, why am I killing myself to exercise when I'm not ready? The other mums didn't say anything, but I felt there was an undertone of comment. Obviously, you see women on social media who seem to get back to normal two weeks after labour. We were all feeling that pressure in the background.'

Like so many things about becoming a mother, our relationship with our body after giving birth is often waaaay more complicated than we expected. As usual, there is a lack of honest information and conversation about what happens and how women feel about it, starting with the extent and variety of changes that we might experience. Weight gain gets a lot of attention but there's also loose skin, stretch marks, varicose veins, a wider ribcage and back, bigger feet, skin problems and hair loss. Not to mention the lack of sexual desire and feeling unattractive and confused about what clothes to wear for a new body and a new role.

If you were relying on mainstream and social media for your info and inspo, you might think that after a woman has a baby, her body, style and confidence will return to being just as they were before – so long as she's disciplined enough to drop the baby weight within a few months and 'bounce back' into her pre-baby jeans. Even though most of us know (because we're not daft) that this isn't quite the full picture, we still get seduced. We're bombarded with images of celebrity and influencer mums looking glossy and sleek, well rested and happy as they pose with toddler or baby. We know rationally that these images are styled and retouched and made possible by a small army of support staff, but they can still feel dispiriting if we're feeling very far from glossy. The countervailing stereotype of the chubby 'slummy mummy' with stained leggings and baby sick in her hair at least takes the pressure off, but it's still playing into the same old stories that society tells about mothers. We're either utterly perfect or failing miserably.

Could there be a more honest, less polarized discussion around the subject? After all, how we experience our body depends on so many more things than what we see in the mirror or what society tells us we should look like. Fundamentals like whether or not we're in pain, or whether we can scramble up a hill or dance round our kitchen on a Friday night. Do we feel content? Do we feel hot? Do we even recognize ourselves in the mirror? What is it really like to live inside a body that might respond very differently after giving birth? What are the gains and losses? What are the surprises about our bodies postpartum?

We asked, and you told us – about everything from pride to disappointment; relief that you no longer have to care about your appearance to a new-found confidence. The variety of experiences is, of course, huge. Many women report feeling dissatisfied with their body postpartum, especially the way it looks; but others say they've never had so much admiration and respect for their body. Some women talk about feeling strong and powerful – amazed by what their body has been capable of. Others talk about feeling fragile, with joint pain and mobility issues they didn't have before.

Your relationship with your body as you move through matrescence will depend on so many unique factors, from your overall health and fitness to your birthing experience and how much support you have from friends, family and health professionals, as well as whether you have the resources to do exercise, eat healthily and get at least *some* sleep. Some of these elements are under your control (or at least will increasingly be under your control as you get a little more time and energy to yourself), but not all of them are. And for all of us, no matter how fortunate our circumstances, there is always the backdrop of society's crazily unrealistic and shaming attitudes to women's bodies.

Dr Lisa Folden works with mothers who are anywhere between six months and 20 years postpartum, to develop a positive relationship with their body. She helps people figure out what a healthy body means *for them*. 'Many of the women I work with say, "I just want to feel better in my body and be able to do certain things again." They're very sincere, but because diet culture is so pervasive everywhere, from our homes to our schools and workplaces, people conflate health with the size, shape or weight of their body. When, in reality, the way your body looks is not a direct reflection of your health status.'

Dr Lisa encourages women to be realistic and self-loving rather than just buying into the latest wellbeing or aesthetic trend. 'Body autonomy is crucial and everyone can and must set their own goals, but it's valuable to recognize that it isn't easy to feel content in a postpartum body. We live in societies that tell us that our status and worth depend on looking a certain way for ever (young, slim, sexy, cis, white, able-bodied and pretty). Having a baby can offer an opportunity to unpick old assumptions and embrace your body as it is right now, but that will take time and effort.' As with so many issues you encounter on your motherhood journey, try to take the long view. Building a positive relationship with your postpartum body might not be straightforward, but it's worth it. And in the meantime, take it easy on yourself.

I am more conscious of the negative things I say about myself and my body now. My rule is: if I wouldn't say it to my daughter(s), I shouldn't say it about myself.

— Kara B., US

187

The upsides, ambivalence and feeling 'meh'

Let's start with some amazing stories of hard-won body positivity. A small but significant minority of women tell us they previously suffered from eating disorders and body dysmorphia, but these issues have been resolved through motherhood. They talk about relating to their body from a new position of acceptance and self-love and wanting to model these attitudes for their children. Katarina P. from Canada, for example, is thinking about how her body will carry her into a future she can share with her daughter. 'I used to have body dysmorphic disorder. I don't know exactly what changed in my brain, but now I can look in the mirror and see the way I really look. I no longer care about my size so long as I look stylish. I want to be strong and live long to watch my daughter grow, thrive, find her dream job, find the love of her life, get married and have kids.'

Or there's Julia O. from the UK, for whom motherhood has made it possible to feel safe in her body as she never did before. 'I used to struggle with an eating disorder and hate my body, but from the very first day I found out I was pregnant, it wasn't about me any more. My body has made two miracles and kept them safe, and I am so so grateful to it. I take care of it with gentleness and respect. My body looks different than before babies, but it feels more like home than ever.'

> I just don't feel bad about the imperfections any more and it's so liberating. I'm proud of what my body did, and all the lumps, bumps and stripes that have come with that.
>
> — Abi W., UK

But you don't need to have suffered with severe body dysmorphia to find the physicality of pregnancy and postpartum transformative and empowering. Many women tell us that they have a deeper relationship with their body now. They no longer obsess over so-called imperfections, and instinctively value and appreciate their body in a more holistic way. One Australia-based mum told us she felt more connected to and appreciative of her body than ever before. She was proud of its ability to bring life safely into the world and had learned to be kinder in the way she viewed it.

Women have profoundly mixed feelings about their body in motherhood. A clear majority feel ambivalent, lamenting some changes while welcoming others. Very often mums miss aesthetic aspects such as the shape of their pre-breastfeeding breasts, while feeling admiration, gratitude and respect for the functional aspects – those breasts fed a child. Or they miss their flat stomach but love their rounded belly or C-scar as a sign of their lived experience and identity as a mother. Jocelyn S. from the US talks about her body evolving, and her sense of wonder combines with nostalgia for what she lost along the way. 'In some ways I am amazed by what it is capable of – what it was able to do without my intentional thought or guidance. It did the work, and beautifully. Other ways, I miss how it used to look, move, feel, before it evolved – twice!'

Many mums seem to be telling themselves to be proud of what their body has done, as a way of consoling themselves for what they perceive as a loss of attractiveness or youthfulness. Kay B. from the UK is typical when she says, 'I know my body did an amazing thing growing a human, but I feel that as a woman, I am spent. I'm no longer a sexual being.' Or Stephanie G., also from the UK, whose distress comes over clearly when she tells us, 'I feel completely disconnected. It's almost not my body any more, more a vessel that's held a baby. Sometimes I am severely upset by how I look but I respect my body for what it has done and try to ignore it for what it cannot do.' It's hardly surprising that we would feel these tensions between pride and disappointment, respect and loss. Living in a woman's body is always complicated, and being postpartum adds another layer of complexity.

Women become more accepting and more positive with the passage of time. Mothers of infants were the most likely to tell us they had strong negative feelings towards their body. Women further along their motherhood journey report both more mixed feelings and more positivity. Whether that's because they've 'bounced back' or have made their peace with their changed body isn't always clear, but it does seem that, for most of us, our relationship with our postpartum body improves with time. We can get fitter and feel stronger; we can heal, rediscover our mojo and libido, and love our body as it is. If that prospect feels remote for you right now, take comfort in the knowledge that things can and will get better.

> *I used to hold so much value in my body. I know now that it will never be how it used to be, but that's okay. My body was beautiful before, incredible when creating and growing my daughter, and now it's a map of what we've been through together.*
>
> **— Rhiana H., UK**

The dark side: disgust and shame

Despite this determination to celebrate their body's strength and appreciate its capacity to nurture a child, there is still a dark side to some women's feelings. Some people feel overwhelmingly negative. The stubborn extra weight, the mummy pouch, loose skin or stretch marks are not just an aesthetic frustration but a blow to their sense of self. There is a genuine sense of loss and mourning for the pre-baby body, and that has a knock-on effect on many other areas of life, from identity to sexuality. Valerie S. from the US, for example, has strongly negative feelings about how her body works *and* how it looks. 'I hate my body now. I'm overweight and weaker than I've ever been. Breastfeeding has changed my breasts significantly, my tummy is saggy and I don't have the time to make myself look cute like I used to. I don't feel like I'm even living in my own body.'

It is an amazing and powerful thing to carry, birth and feed a child, and women still receive far too little real appreciation and support for this physically and emotionally demanding work. And yet, when we celebrate the changes to our postpartum body as battle scars that demonstrate our achievement, do we risk seeing ourselves as a failure if we couldn't carry a healthy pregnancy to term, give birth as we wanted to, breastfeed our child, then bounce back within weeks? If our body can 'succeed' and make us proud, can it also 'fail'?

Women who have suffered miscarriages, or whose children are born premature or with health or developmental problems, sometimes carry a terrible and unfair burden of guilt and shame due to problematic beliefs about a body's capacity for success and failure. We know that for far too many mums, a C-section or formula feeding are experienced as failure. So is ending up with a body that doesn't resemble your pre-pregnancy self and being unable to do anything about it. The emotional effects and impact on our sense of who we are can be devastating.

Dr Lisa Folden has very clear thoughts on the shame that mothers carry because of beliefs about their body. 'As women we're born into a system that tells us our bodies are designed to conceive, carry and birth a healthy child. That's what we're *supposed* to do and so much of a woman's value is still attached to it. Which means that if your body can't, for whatever reason, give birth vaginally or breastfeed, or your child has additional needs or health problems, then you might need to hear that you are no less valuable and no less worthy. We are *all* worthy.'

We sure are. Every mother is worthy of respect and appreciation from loved ones and society at large. We are all worthy of our own self-love. And yet it's in very short supply. Katarina A. from the US said something heartbreaking about her relationship with her body after three kids. 'I still don't like my body. It's not even about the mom pouch at seven months postpartum after my third. It's that I can't get off the couch without peeing myself. It's that I'm killing myself trying to exercise and it's not helping. Every doctor has been so dis-missive because "Oh, you've had three kids. Just do kegels."'

If this is you, and you've been suffering with incontinence, pelvic pain, diastasis recti, persistent alienation from or dislike of your body – please go to see a (sympathetic) health pro-fessional. You could start with your GP or primary doctor, who might refer you to a specialist. Try a CBT therapist or a counsellor if you're struggling with negative self-image, or seek out a specialist in postpartum therapies if you have pain and other physical symptoms. There are pelvic floor trainers and women's health physios who treat women with a range of issues. There are also self-help programmes online, such as Mutu, which are proven to help with pelvic pain and less severe abdominal diastasis. Nobody needs to put up with birth injuries, pain or body dysmorphia. There is help available. You deserve it.

I've always struggled with how I see myself. Pregnancy (in a sense) has allowed me to reconcile with my own body and accept that every human is different and that is beautiful.

— Clarissa F., US

Beyond the body – new brain, new life, new style

We often think first about visible (negatively perceived) changes to the postpartum body – the extra weight, the stretch marks, mummy pouch after a C-section, etc. But even if you came to motherhood without carrying and birthing a baby, your biology will still be altered by your experience of matrescence. In 2022, a team led by Winnie Orchard, a neuroscientist at Yale University, analyzed all the available studies on brain connectivity in matrescence. They found evidence that the structure of your brain will undergo changes as you care for your new child, whether they're a baby or older. Circuits that connect areas of your brain involved in pleasure and reward, empathy and hypervigilance are all strengthened through rewiring. These brain changes take place in *any* primary caregiver, not just the mother who has birthed the child. Mothers who adopt their children, fathers, foster carers – anyone who spends enough time interacting with a baby will display measurable changes in brain function as they develop greater sensitivity to the baby's needs. It seems that motherhood's physical changes don't stop at weight gain and stretch marks – plus, they're not even confined to mothers.

Lots of mums sense that they're more forgetful or easily distracted than they were before they had their children. Setting aside the point that being sleep-deprived will definitely do that to anyone, mummy brain *is* a phenomenon that scientists can observe at a neurological level. It happens as a result of those intensive renovations to make our brain fit for purpose in this new phase of our life. But rather than thinking of it as a loss of the thinking capacity we had before, it makes more sense to think of it as a gain. In time, and with more sleep, brain fog clears. But a mother (or primary carer's) extra empathy and emotional intelligence stick around much longer. Mummy brain is a real thing – but not in the way we're often told.

The changes to our body and brain affect our identity in so many complex ways, including how we present ourselves to the world through clothes and make-up. It can be a shock to realize that you no longer know what you want to wear, or what you think you should wear, especially if style and appearance have been important to you. Whether the confusion is due to a changed body shape or not knowing how to dress for the new role of being somebody's mother, it's an issue that came up a lot when we asked about how women perceive their appearance in motherhood.

Lots of people report feeling they've lost their sense of style because their old wardrobe doesn't fit them any more, both literally and figuratively. We hear from lifelong style fiends who now hate clothes shopping.

There's definitely an element of fearing judgement from other people. Women say they sense an expectation that they must dress a certain (more practical, less sexy) way once they become a mother, and sometimes that's in tension with what society expects women to wear, and what they want to wear themselves. Sometimes the expectations come from other mums. 'I am more self-conscious now when I'm picking out outfits,' says Danielle M. 'Sometimes I worry that I'm not dressed like other moms. I feel "too fancy" if I'm wearing jeans, a T-shirt and a pair of heels when all the other moms are in flats and leggings.'

It's hardly surprising that what we wear as mums can end up feeling tribal. Anyone who's ever been a teenage girl knows that clothes, make-up and hair send messages about who you want to be and who you want to hang out with. Style can be a fun form of self-expression, or about fitting in, hiding away or standing out. It sums up how you feel about your body and yourself, your past and your present, your self-hood as a woman and a mother. No wonder it's complicated. Of all the ways that mums have to bond, sympathize, commiserate and support one another – or not – sharing their feelings over their new body can be one of the most powerful. Postpartum bodies shouldn't be treated as places of competition between women but embraced as symbols of what we all have in common. Nurturing our new body is self-care. How much more radical and powerful if we can do that alongside other women, in the gym, the park, the spa, the changing room, or our best friend's clothes swap party? A village of women showing love and appreciation of their own and other's bodies . . . bring it on.

In a nutshell . . .

Can you find a cheerleader who can help you to celebrate and care for yourself? They might be a supportive partner, a friend, a therapist or a fitness instructor – anyone who can remind you that you put your body on the line to bring a child into being, and you deserve to celebrate and care for yourself.

Building a healthy relationship with your new body is a fantastic aim but it's worth taking some time to figure out what that means to you. Too often we hear people say they want to be 'healthy' when what we know they still mean, deep down, is 'slimmer'. It can help to put the emphasis on your relationship with your body, which is a work in progress, rather than the outcome, which too often comes with a whole load of stereotypical baggage.

Being a role model for your children offers an opportunity to practise body positivity, self-acceptance and self-love. This will take time to feel authentic. Give yourself the grace to grow into a different relationship with your body and don't beat yourself up if you occasionally fall back on less positive habits.

Curate your social media feeds to surround yourself with genuine body positivity and healthy realism. There's no doubt that social media can damage our body image and sense of self, especially when we're feeling vulnerable. Be mindful of how you react to certain accounts. If you consistently feel envious, guilty or ashamed, take that as a warning and unfollow.

CHAPTER 14

Shouldn't this be getting easier?

On slow progress and avoiding burnout

Pick any ongoing struggle related to the transition into motherhood, from poor sleep to lack of friends, and you can absolutely guarantee that thousands of other women are also asking themselves whether it's ever going to get any easier. 'I didn't expect it to take this long.' That's Becca A. on feeling comfortable again in her postpartum body. 'I didn't expect sleep to be so rough for so long.' That's Claudia T. 'It's taken years to find good friends. So much longer than I expected.' That's Kirsty W. 'It's been a journey to get back to wanting to be intimate with my husband. It's another thing that took way longer than I expected.' Becca A. again.

Even if you feel that you and your child are coping reasonably well, you're probably also discovering that there's always a new challenge coming down the track. You just figured out breastfeeding and suddenly you're on to weaning. Finally get a sleep schedule together and your child gets sick, or you go back to work and everything's up in the air again. Plus, as we've said before, the world doesn't stop just because you're a mother now. There will always be big life events that impact you and your family. You might lose your job. You might split from your partner. Life can feel relentless; life in motherhood, doubly so.

Kerry Tay is from the UK but lives in Colorado. We met her back in Chapter Three. She describes the first year of her son's life as 'one thing after another. We were barely done with one big issue and then there would be something else to cope with. First there was having to move across the world in a desperate hurry because of Covid lockdowns, then my father was diagnosed with cancer and I didn't get to see him before he died. The depression and loneliness were awful and I just bottled it all up until Zander was born, when it came back stronger. Three months postpartum, Zander got very sick with RSV, a respiratory illness that mainly affects children, and he had to go into ICU. It was only a week, but it was terrifying. I started to feel very anxious. Also, I spent months trying to establish breastfeeding, only for us to find out when he was nine months that he had a tongue tie. By then I had exclusively pumped milk for five months, so I was very tired. I was grieving my dad and missing my mum. That whole year felt like a slog and I started to wonder if life would ever get easier. It did eventually. We figured out Zander's feeding and my mum was finally able to visit. We're now settled and well. But it took longer than I ever would have expected.'

If you're deep into your child's first year and you're wondering why motherhood isn't feeling easier yet and whether the problem is you, please take heart from all these women's voices. You're not doing it wrong and there's no timetable you and your baby 'should' be following. It's just a uniquely tough gig, remember? Kerry and her family are 'absolutely fine now'. Her words. So are Becca A. and Kirsty W. Claudia's still struggling, which is tough. Adjusting to the reality of your new life is like any other complex and important task: it takes time, effort, patience and a lot of trial and error. Thinking in terms of how it 'should' be is only likely to heap more pressure on.

This chapter is about how to keep your spirits up when a new issue rears its head or a familiar problem resurfaces. It might be the complicated feelings that come along with your baby's development, such as when you decide to stop breastfeeding. It might be chronic loneliness, as initial involvement from friends drops away and you realize that your old social life is not coming back. Or the anxiety that can crop up when you're meeting new mum friends and chatting about your children, which can be fertile ground for comparisons, competitiveness and resentment.

Mums are especially vulnerable to burnout round about now, as accumulated tiredness combines with the relentless work of mothering to produce emotional exhaustion. Self-care passes from being a nice-to-have to an absolute priority, but how can you make sure you squeeze it in? We're here to show you how mums have navigated these difficulties to arrive at their child's first birthday with sanity and spirit intact.

Missing your tiny baby even though you love seeing them grow up

It can be a sad–sweet feeling to realize that your gorgeous baby is heading for toddlerhood. Obviously there will be huge delight as they continue to learn new skills and you get to know them more and more, but many women also talk about missing each stage of their baby's life as it passes. The teeny newborn who clung to your finger is never coming back, which is awesome because you get to meet the walking talking child they're on their way to becoming, and yet it can still feel poignant. These complex feelings of joy and nostalgia often come to a peak around issues like breastfeeding, which is so emotive and intimate, and which, at some point, you will decide to stop. That process can be deeply emotional. For those mums who have enjoyed breastfeeding, stopping is often a wrench – even if we know there will be benefits in terms of personal autonomy. Some of us have become dependent on feeding to comfort our child, so having to find other ways, especially as they relate to sleeping at night, is another huge challenge.

Kylie H. from Northern California talked to us about how weaning was hard for her, partly because breastfeeding was a great tool for comforting her son and also because she was emotionally attached to it. 'It was almost the only time he wanted to cuddle with me. He's super-active, loves to run around and play, would much rather be doing that than sleeping or eating solid food, so I loved the feeding and the cuddles . . . But he was becoming quite emotionally dysregulated around feeding for comfort. We would be out in public and if he got upset, he would be asking for boob, boob, and pulling my shirt open. So I had to find other ways to comfort him, with a fruit snack or a little video on Dada's phone. It was time, basically. We were done.'

Once she'd decided it was time to stop, Kylie tapered breastfeeds down over a number of weeks. She fed her son for the last time just after he turned two. 'I explained that I had loved nursing him but that he was ready to stop feeding from me because there were so many things he could eat now. I was going to go away for a couple of nights to stay at a friend's so this would be our last time and when I came back, there would be no more. He's asked a couple of times since, when he's been upset, but I think I've found it harder than he has!'

Loneliness, old friends and new connections

At some point in the second half of your baby's first year, you might look around and wonder where your old friends have gone. A lot of mums experience sadness, confusion and even heartbreak connected to their old friendships dissolving after they become parents. For every mum like Tricia C. from the US, who tells us, 'It's been pretty solid with my friends. We still get together whenever we can and they're very support-ive,' there are five or six who say something like, 'My friends have stopped inviting me to things, assuming I wouldn't want to go. There's much less contact in general and one of my closest friends has become distant.'

It's great to hear from women like Tricia that their social lives are holding up and their old friends are rallying around, but it's also important to recognize that many women feel for-gotten. Women use words like 'neglected' and 'abandoned'. It's not just that they feel let down if friends don't rush round to help out. The pain is deeper than that. They feel over-looked and unseen, as if motherhood has erased them from friendship's map.

Losing friends as we shift into motherhood doesn't get talked about much. It can feel shameful, as if we aren't good enough for people to want to stay in our lives. The pain and shock of a close friendship falling apart can feel like being dumped, and it hurts when old friends seem to have no interest in meeting your child. It's more likely if you're out of sync with your social circle – either the first to have a child or much later than all your friends, but it happens to women in every different situation.

Some mums are stoical, recognizing that if our life choices diverge from those of our friends it's not surprising that people will fall away. Plenty of others report that they themselves want to move away from old friends because their values no longer align. Jordan S. said, 'I'm closer with some friends, especially those who have children, but I feel estranged from one of my friendship groups. I don't have the energy or drive to live their lifestyle any more. I don't disagree with their choices, but I have moved on to the next stage of my life.'

Even if values are still in sync, your own energy, time and money are likely to be much tighter than before you had your child. Sometimes this means that friendships take a temporary dip, but so long as communication stays warm and open there's no reason they can't be picked up later.

The most damaging thing for women is to feel they've been dropped suddenly, just because they became a mother. When there's no acknowledgement of what's happened, and especially if the individual was a really close or longstanding friend, the hurt can be huge and can make it difficult to trust people in the future. If that dynamic is combined with difficulties in making new friends, a spiral of isolation can set in.

If you're spiralling right now, please take heart. There may be no quick fixes to loneliness, but with time and persistence, you will find new friends to replace those you have lost. Kirsty W. has some very grounding thoughts on this. 'If I could give my younger self one piece of advice, it would be to manage my expectations. Not to expect that I'll make five besties in the first six months of being a mom, or even the first year. New moms have so much on their plate, so they come and go in your life. It's good not to take that social ebb and flow so personally.' As Kirsty says, those connections take longer to build when you have your hands full with a baby. It's tough to hear things like 'you'll meet new friends when your child starts nursery, or school' if that's still a year or more away, but maybe the comfort lies in the message that there will always be another opportunity to meet someone you can connect with.

The Sticky Stuff:
Comparisons, opinionated mums and feeling judged

When we're interacting with people who have children the same age as ours, we're naturally going to chat about what we have in common – our babies, and everything from the crazy noises they make when they're falling asleep to whether or not they're sitting up yet. There's nothing wrong with that, but these chats can quickly become stressful if we get stuck in the comparison trap, comparing our child with someone else's. Most mums are not showing off about their child's amazing sitting-up abilities, they're just excited; and yet if we're worried about our own child, it can grate on us. The spiral from seed of concern to full-blown anxiety and inadequacy can be very quick.

As well as the anxiety, there's also a shame and guilt component to these difficult conversations. At some point, practically every mama in our community has

experienced the sting of feeling that their approach to
motherhood is being judged and found wanting. We've
already talked about some of the classic pinch points
that might lead to these uncomfortable feelings, such as
breastfeeding or working outside the home, but there
are lots of situations where we end up feeling a little
criticized. Sometimes it's not overt, it's more the result
of having conversations with opinionated people, which
can bring on massive self-doubt.

Joanna D. adopted her two children and they've
only recently joined the family full-time after a period
transitioning away from foster care. 'At playgroup some
people have said my daughter should be at nursery by
now, otherwise she won't be ready for school. I don't
think people mean anything bad by it, but they can be
very quick to share their opinions. That stresses me
out because I worry that I'm setting the children up for
failure. I don't necessarily have the energy to explain
our situation, and that we're prioritizing bonds with
me and my husband for now. Sometimes I just duck a
conversation. I feel self-conscious and anxious about
being judged, even when I tell myself that it's probably
mostly just my perception.' Joanna is generous in
recognizing that part of the responsibility for coping
with these situations lies with her, but as she rightly says,
it's not always easy to stay calm when you're tired or a
topic is sensitive.

The comparisons, opinions and judgements can
feel especially toxic when they're coming up with
your siblings, for example. Different approaches

to parenting often reflect family dynamics from a previous generation, as Danielle B. from Canada recognized. 'My brother is a completely different parent than I am. He's protective and careful, too much so in my opinion. Those kids have very little freedom to fail or get hurt . . . And I know how detrimental that was to my development, as our father was similar.' Each of us brings so much baggage to our parenting choices, our relationships and our reactions in the moment. It's easy to end up communicating in ways that make another person feel criticized, even if we don't intend to.

So what helps? How can we all do our best not to take on feelings of being judged or giving the impression to other mums that we are sitting in judgement?

If we feel confident in our choices, we're less susceptible to anxious comparisons or to feeling criticized. It's tricky to be confident all the time, especially when we're learning how to do something so important, but having a 'good enough' mindset really helps. Remember, there's no such thing as the perfect solution, outcome, child or mother. Doing what works for you and your child is *absolutely* good enough. Figuring out what works through trial and error is fine. Cath F. from the US sums up this calm and open mindset when she says, 'Assume the best intentions when someone is sharing their opinion. Listen to everyone's advice, take anything useful, take the rest with a pinch of salt and then do what works best for you.'

More compassion for our own insecurities and other people's can make a big difference. As Veronica Cisneros remarks, 'It's easy to fall into old insecurities when comparing ourselves to another mom. Take a breath and ask yourself who you want to be in this situation, or this moment. We're bound to feel insecure if we've never actually identified what we want and what our values are. We can be much more confident even when we don't know the answers, if we're at least asking the right questions with kindness.'

Listening more carefully and slowing down our comments so we can assess how they might land is always a good idea. 'My sister listens to me when I'm ranting,' says Daniela O. 'She really hears me. I don't think I could have managed this past year without her.' Taking the pressure off and aiming to be as relaxed as possible helped for Claire S. from the UK, when she made a small group of mum friends through a baby class. 'We're all quite different but it was just nice to meet non-judgemental mums at a similar stage of life. We can get together with the babies, embrace the chaos and have a cup of tea!' This speaks to something we know makes a huge difference to many women, which is trying to distinguish between treating motherhood as important (which it is) and taking it too seriously (which can really sap the joy and lead to stress).

Joanna D. told us a story about an interaction at the same playgroup where she had previously felt insecure and judged. 'The loveliest thing happened: I met a mum recently who's been so supportive. She bought me a cup of tea, we got chatting. She didn't ask loads of questions about adoption, she approached it really sensitively. She said things like, "I'm sorry if I've said that wrong" and "If there's something you don't want to talk about, let me know". Her parenting style is quite different from mine but there's a mutual respect there. It's like, *You do it that way, I don't judge. I just do it my way.*' Amen to that.

Mum burnout and the importance of genuine self-care

Nyah G. from Australia says she barely does anything for herself. 'I will hand the kids off to my partner when he gets home, but then I'm still doing housework.' When we asked what she does for fun, she replied ironically, 'Does watching *Paw Patrol* with my toddler count?' She mentioned lack of personal space, time, money, energy and childcare as factors that prevent her from looking after herself, and these barriers are cited by the majority of women who say they struggle to fulfil their own needs. There's no doubt that when resources of time and money are scarce, it's mums who go short. If you're a single parent without support, for example, it can feel as if life is set to constant grind. Between work, household tasks and caring for your child, there's nothing left.

There might be another barrier. If you don't feel worthy of boosting yourself to the top of the priority list from time to time, then you're going to struggle to justify time away from your family's needs. And yet mums deserve fun as well as rest. They need calm as well as stimulation, creativity as

well as nurturing. There are as many ways to look after ourselves as there are different mamas out there, but the crucial
thing is to allow yourself that space and time – even if it's only
a few minutes a day – to do something that benefits only you.

Physical therapist Dr Lisa Folden says most women are
doing self-care all wrong. Rather than fulfilling their own
needs first and constantly, then allowing their abundant
wellness to spill over to others, they're pouring out all their
energies while struggling to replenish them. She had to learn
this herself, when she was on the edge of burnout. 'I had
spent years trying to be the perfect mom, until one day I just
couldn't carry on. I realized that my kids don't need "the
perfect mom", they need an honest, healthy mom – mentally,
emotionally, spiritually. From there everything started to
change.'

Dr Lisa invites mums to think of themselves as being 'like
a big glass with little glasses around you. Most of us go to
the sink, fill up our glass and then pour and pour into all the
little glasses. When we get empty, we go back to the sink. We
do this over and over again. We give ourselves just enough
care to give it away. And that's if we're being good and filling
ourselves up first. Some people aren't even doing that. What
I try to do instead is, I set my glass on top of those small
glasses and I take that faucet and run it. As I overflow, I pour
into them. So I never go empty. This applies to however you
define your self-care, right? Some days it's paying your bills.
Some days it's a spa day. Some days it's sleeping in. Some days
it's staying up late. Fulfilling your own needs and prioritizing
your own goals looks different in any moment. What we're
talking about really is radical self-love.'

As Dr Lisa says, it's not even that you deserve it. It's that
you and your family also *need* it, because otherwise you're

running the risk of mum burnout. 'You can't keep depleting yourself. I mean, you *can* for a season or two, but you're going to be run down. You're going to be unhappy. And you're setting an example for your children that this is how they show their worth – by putting on everybody else's oxygen mask first, and then hopefully getting to theirs before they pass out. I want my kids to take very good care of themselves so that they have the energy and the wherewithal to take care of others.'

This season of motherhood is a tough one. As the months of disrupted sleep and the emotional roller coaster of caring for your child take a toll, your resilience is being depleted. You might have gone back to paid work and are now doing the working parent's double shift. You might be readying to go back or realizing that you can't or don't want to. Whatever your circumstances, it's common to be doubting yourself as a mother, questioning whether you're good enough, feeling irritable, snappy and guilty. Some of us are feeling frazzled and lost by this point, struggling to connect with our children or other loved ones.

If that's you, please take a moment to consider whether you might be approaching burnout. If you think you are, now is the perfect moment to pause, reflect on what small changes you could make, and ask for help. Start with things you can do yourself, such as including specific activities in your day or repeating positive affirmations such as 'I am a good mother and I'm doing a good job'. That can help to calm you in the moment and empower you by reconnecting with your core resilience.

It's also worth talking to a friend or family member honestly about how you're feeling, making an appointment with a doctor or a therapist, or dropping into an online parents' forum. Feeling that we can't cope with motherhood or dreading being with our kids is a horrible sensation that is guaranteed to reinforce our negative emotions. There's no shame in admitting to these feelings and asking for help. Mothering is not a one-woman job and if you're struggling, please reach out, even if – especially if – that feels like admitting weakness or failure.

> I've worked in the emergency department of a hospital, doing back-to-back cardiac arrests and endless night shifts. Having kids is harder. The stress, the emotional strain, the exhaustion and the potential for burnout are always there. It's crucial to accept that we need help.
> — **Dr Zoya, UK, doctor and mother of twins**

Mitra N. from London has interesting thoughts about finding it hard to ask for help, and to accept help with self-compassion as well as gratitude. 'I think many of us have swallowed this idea that, as an adult, you have to be completely self-sufficient at all times. It's seen as infantilizing to ask for help from family or friends. Perhaps because of my South Asian background, I don't see life like that. I think it's normal to ask for help during difficult periods. It doesn't make me less of an adult to need and want my mum to help me with my children.'

It takes a village, remember? So if you're feeling the frazzle, be kind to yourself. Prioritize your wellbeing. Allow yourself to feel worthy of care. That's the fastest way back to being able to care for your child and your family. And one day, when it's another mum's turn to feel frazzled, you'll be in a great position to help.

Some situations are so challenging that it can feel almost trivial to talk about self-care in the same breath, and yet when you're in crisis, it's even more vital to look after yourself, accept help and pull together as a village. Stefani C.'s son is eight months old and has spent six months of his life in hospital, much of it sedated. Matteo has a heart condition, floppy muscle syndrome and a tracheostomy tube.

'He's home now and he's doing better,' Stefani tells us in a calm voice and with a bright smile, 'but he's a high-risk baby. I'm a nurse by training so although taking care of him is challenging, I adapted to it really fast. It's different when it's your own child, though. Before I had him I had a different picture of how motherhood was going to be, but you know, he's just a beautiful little boy. When he wakes up, his monitors start to go off and he laughs. He has this beautiful smile where he shows me his little teeth and tries to chat away to me. I chat back to him and we both end up laughing.

'I know Matteo so well now. I feel confident that we can do this together. Even if I'd known what was coming before I had him, I wouldn't change a thing. But I couldn't have done it without my fiancé, Sergio, and our family. They've been so loving and have given us every help. Sergio insists I look after myself and I know I need to, for everyone's sake. I prioritize taking time to relax and get out and about to do things.'

Stefani clearly deserves all the support, understanding, care, relaxation and time to be herself that she could possibly want. *Every* mum deserves those things. The struggles we face are different, but we're all working hard to create a deep bond with our child, build an understanding of their needs and get comfortable with our new role. We all want to get to our child's first birthday with a growing sense of confidence, looking forward to whatever comes next.

Let yourself celebrate everything you've done and learned. Whatever your ongoing challenges, you and your child have come a long way together. As Dr Lisa says, 'Our society constantly pushes us to achieve more, and while it's great to work to be the best version of you, it's also important to be able to stop: smell the roses, enjoy the progress, revel in where you are.' Mamas can be their own toughest critics. We're so quick to hear and amplify criticisms and we struggle to accept compliments, kindness and encouragement. If you find yourself longing for life to be easier, please take small steps to ease up on yourself. Invite your village to come closer. And remember that simply by showing up every day for your family in good faith, you are doing a great job.

In a nutshell . . .

If motherhood is still feeling tough, that doesn't mean it will never get easier. This is a long journey of adaptation and a hard job you're doing. Savour moments of joy with your child and look for ways to feel joyful apart from them. Motherhood is a story of extremes – don't forget to enjoy the highs as well as reassuring yourself that the lows will pass.

You are doing a great job at figuring out how to be a mum. Whatever the persistent struggle you're coping with, whether it's fatigue, loneliness, battles with loved ones, strains with a partner or feeling anxious about your approach to motherhood, remember that you don't need to be perfect, you just need to be yourself. Stop comparing, judging and criticizing – yourself or anyone else.

Self-care is a necessity, not a luxury. Never feel guilty for prioritizing yourself. Remember, your children will benefit in so many ways when you do. And take your own wellbeing seriously, from health to fun. Try making lists of different enjoyable and nourishing activities that require varying amounts of time, energy and money. They could vary from a ten-minute pause with a meditation app to getting your nails done. It also helps to categorize them into non-negotiables, nice-to-haves and aspirational treats.

PART FIVE
Looking ahead

CHAPTER 15

Is this who I am now?

On what we lose and what we gain –
ambivalence and adjustment

Becoming a mother knocks a woman off her feet in a hurricane of love, tears, hormones and tiredness. It's no wonder so many of us spend the first year or so feeling a little battered. Once the waters are calmer there's an opportunity to look around and ask ourselves: who am I now? What remains of the old version of myself and how can I reconnect with some aspects and let go of others? How do I integrate being a mama alongside all my other roles and identities? And how can I figure it all out, gently and with self-compassion?

When we asked the Peanut community how motherhood had impacted on their sense of identity, hundreds of them responded. While almost everyone felt changed, there was a huge variety of responses. Some people talked about transformation, others about completion. Many mamas spoke of self-discovery and empowerment. We heard words like 'matriarch', 'superhero' and 'protector' and we heard over and over again that women felt more important and more purposeful, more mature and self-reliant. We also heard about 'getting lost' in motherhood and being erased by it. Kara B. from the US told us, 'To be completely transparent, my whole identity has become being a mother. I have totally lost myself in the process.'

It's no wonder many of us feel disorientated by motherhood when it wipes away a lot of the reference points we use to understand ourselves. If you've always thought of yourself as someone who works hard and plays hard, let's say, or who loves adventurous travel or is focused on the next promotion at work, or needs a lot of alone time, or a lot of time with friends, then becoming a mother is going to cut you off from those ways in which you feel like yourself. Whether you're an introverted homebody or an extroverted party girl, whether you live for your creative hobby or know that being in the gym five days a week is non-negotiable for your mental health, becoming a mother means you have less time and energy to be anything else. That's hard. It's tough not to get your needs met, even if you knew it was going to happen. It's perhaps even harder to feel that you don't know who you are any more, or that your old self is lost to you or invisible to other people.

> It is hard taking care of a human being 24/7, we all know
> that, but in my opinion it is harder to mourn a life you will
> no longer have, and be okay with that. Being a mom is
> one of the best things that has ever happened to me
> but also one of the most traumatic experiences I've ever
> had. I've learned to accept that.
>
> — Clarissa F., US

There are key themes that come up over and over again, to do with shifting priorities, losses and sacrifices as well as unexpected gains – especially to women's sense of purpose. When asked about these changes, 40 per cent of people said that on balance the changes were broadly positive, 38 per cent had mixed feelings, and for 22 per cent, the impact had been felt in mainly negative ways. Of those who were broadly negative, 62 per cent had children under one year old. Only 8 per cent of parents to children of preschool age were still reporting that they felt negative overall. 'It gets easier' is a truism that's borne out by the general trend of lived experience. Clodagh N. from Ireland put it like this: 'The newborn stage was all-consuming. I was only a mother. Now, at nearly nine months postpartum, I feel being a parent has completed me. I still have my own identity and I'm just so much more content in myself.'

How *you* feel about this huge and complex question of your new identity and role in life is obviously unique to you. There are no right ways to be a mother and there's certainly no right way to be you. Virtually every mama struggles with some aspect of her identity as she transitions into motherhood, and the timing and triggers for these periods of questioning will be different for everyone. Let's work through the Peanut community's collective wisdom on navigating the losses, the gains, the ambivalence and the journey to a new, integrated, even more multi-layered version of yourself.

> I feel I've evolved. I've got one side of me that's mom and another that is returning to being more as I was before. The two are merging together to make a new me, as I am now. I feel like a Pokémon!
>
> — **Kerry T., US**

The struggles, ambivalence and amazing gains

'I knew that my world was going to revolve around them but, even so, being a mum is now my whole identity. I'm like their slave. Also, the only thing people ask is how the kids are. Nobody asks about me.' That's Joanna D., whose adopted children have been living with her and her husband for almost four months. They're not babies, they're three and four years old, but motherhood is new to Joanna and she's deep in the loss of her old identity and rapid adjustment to the new.

Disorientation, feeling alienated from yourself and grieving a life that you no longer have are all very common as we move into motherhood. While these feelings may be strongest at the beginning of our journey, they don't necessarily or simply resolve with time. Katie N. from the UK told us that she didn't recognize herself after the birth of her two children and was still grieving the life and the identity she had before them. 'My second child was conceived eight weeks postpartum, so I was just obliterated by tiredness for years. I loved them so intensely but also, I didn't recognize myself any more. I was mourning what I'd lost: my freedom, the lack of anxiety, my identity, having a guilt-free career.' One UK-based mum told us that she felt becoming a mother had split her into two people: the real her and the mum version of her.

As well as the internal confusion so many of us feel, we're also coming to terms with a new external identity. The way the wider world perceives us has just been stripped down to one monolithic identity: being somebody's mother. As Kay B. says, 'Motherhood is amazing, but it's also made me feel less human. Sometimes people treat me as just Atlas's mum, when there's a lot more to me than that.'

And, of course, we're dealing with the external labelling and our internal confusion at the same time. The two things make each other harder to deal with. It's hardly surprising if some of us end up feeling resentful. 'I used to be a performer, a comedian, a singer and a friend. Now I am nothing but a mom to a toddler. Parenting is letting things die inside you to bring forth a child,' said Angel S. from the US, a stay-at-home mum who longs to get back into the workforce and misses freedom, fun with friends, exploring different things, making her own money and spontaneous trips with her boyfriend. 'Just . . . life in general.' Our heart breaks for Angel, who is very socially isolated and struggling with her mental health. She's far from being alone in this phase of frustration and grief.

Given all of this complexity, a high degree of ambivalence about motherhood is almost the norm among parents of babies and toddlers. Thirty-eight per cent of respondents to our survey said things like: 'It was magical and humbling but also sacrificial and erasing.' That's Stephanie W. from the US, who told us that while she had always wanted to be a mum, 'and it's amazing to have that responsibility and opportunity, it's also a lot of work, not just in their care but in maintaining my own sense of self. It can be very lonely, even with a lot of support.' Stephanie is a stay-at-home mum who's now home-schooling her older child as well as looking after her toddler. She misses spontaneity but loves 'how my partnership with my spouse grew, the pitter-patter of feet down the hallway and showing my kids the things I loved when I was a kid'.

Kate M. from the US has a toddler and is honest about the ongoing reality of maternal ambivalence. 'I love her so much, but sometimes I can't stand her. It doesn't last long, thankfully, but I do struggle. A lot of the time I feel like someone's mom rather than Kate. Motherhood has given me a whole new purpose and yet I've also lost so much – freedom and spontaneity, feeling rested and being on top of my game at work. But as much as life can feel exhausting and frustrating, I guess I do feel more fulfilled knowing this kind of love. I just don't think I've wrapped my head around who I am and what my life is now.'

The sense of purpose and deep love that Kate mentions are watchwords for mums talking about their new sense of self. Emily from the US describes her clear sense of mission. 'My role in life now is to raise well-rounded, loving children and make sure they have a good life and happy memories. I've got a job to do.' For women like Andeanna O. from the US, motherhood has given her a meaning and purpose she didn't have before. 'Every time I look in my daughter's eyes, I see that I'm her whole world and she is mine. Before becoming a parent, I didn't know what my identity was. Now it's very clear.'

> I used to be very passive about how others treated me but now I defend myself against my family's criticism and take responsibility for myself as well as my child. I've become a completely different person over these last three years. And I'm proud of myself.
>
> — Daisy V.-V., US

Many women told us they felt deep pride and self-worth, sometimes for the first time in their lives. Anastasia K. from the US said, 'Becoming a mother made me feel like an actual person, which seems kinda silly, but I spent my whole life feeling very disposable and this has made me realize I'm not. That realization changes a lot of things. I was 18 years old and unemployed when I fell pregnant. Now I'm planning to go back to school as soon as I can.' Or as Andeanna put it, 'I see myself as a powerful woman now. Giving life to my child has shown me that I am more than capable of achieving my dreams and aspirations.'

Values shift alongside priorities. Many mums say they no longer want to get distracted by trivia or worrying about what other people think. Life feels simpler for many of us, as if it has been reduced to essentials. As Roslynn W. says, 'I'm bolder and more resolute now. I no longer sweat the small stuff or put up with foolishness as I did when I was younger.' People let go of workaholism and feel more relaxed, despite the undoubted strain of caring for their children. And *so* many women say they laugh *so* much more than they used to. Laughter, joy, discovery and play are all important and often unexpected elements in women's new lives. 'The silliness and joy my kids bring to my life is irreplaceable,' says Sneha S. from Canada. Or as Kylie H. put it, 'There's so much less sleep and personal autonomy in my life, but infinitely more laughter.'

Mothers make countless sacrifices in their daily lives, but the flipside of losing some of yourself is the potential to gain a deeper connection with other people – your children, your family and community. Mums talk about loss and grief but also about how much they have to be thankful for. They use words like 'gift' and 'opportunity'.

We love that so many of us have found growth through motherhood. We love the joy that shines through in the words women use about what becoming a mother means to them. We know that this journey can be transformative in many rich and unexpected ways, just as it can also be crushing and obliterating, and we know that there is nothing like having your village by your side to help you on your way.

The journey to adjustment

If you're not yet enjoying the journey as much as you would like, that's fine. Being a mum is complicated. We know this — and yet many of us still pretend we're finding it easy when we're not, or finding it fulfilling every single day when it isn't. Whether you are months or years into your motherhood journey, being the most complete version of yourself depends on accepting your feelings, doubts and questions. Try to set aside any expectations, including your own, around how mothers *ought* to be. There's still too much weight placed on behaving a certain way, and so many of us struggle to reconcile these simplistic 'shoulds' with our own unique realities.

Remember the voices of all the women you've just been reading. Women who are grateful for motherhood but also feel guilty about their hunger to get back to work, or to write music again, or go for Sunday brunch with friends. Remember, there is no requirement to love being a mother every day in order to be *a good enough mother to the child you love*. You are allowed to be yourself, in all your glorious messy complexity. Or not to have a clue who you are any more and need some time to figure that out.

So what helps on your journey away from confusion towards adjustment? Well, once you've admitted your doubts and fears, you can set about dealing with them. Peanut Pro and confidence coach Darcel Being works with mums to move them towards acceptance of their full selves, using cognitive behavioural principles to help them 'change the belief, in order to change the behaviour, in order to change who they're becoming and who they're being, as a mom and as their whole self'.

Darcel uses the example of a mum who's struggling with a lot of self-doubt. She's anxious about her choice to adopt gentle parenting when her own mother is highly critical of the approach. 'I always invite the person to first acknowledge what's coming up for them. Acknowledge the fear, the doubt, the anxiety. Typically there's a lot of dissonance. In this example, the woman might fear she's making the wrong decisions, because her mom is so much more experienced. But part of her comes back with the thought that, actually, perhaps it's her mom who's wrong. It's a lot to handle so it's no surprise that self-doubt wins out.

'I would invite her to lean into accepting that she is choosing these feelings of being wrong, being anxious. It's a place of victimhood. Why is that? Nine out of ten times the woman says, "It just feels familiar, because growing up my mom always made me feel like I was wrong. The church or my community or my culture always made me feel wrong." When people understand that they're reacting to and feeding an old pattern, they're more able to shift.

'And then the third step is always action. So yes, you've acknowledged it. Yes, you're accepting the role that you are playing. And now you get to shift into radical action. That always looks like something for yourself rather than trying to change the other person. You're going to change something that *you're* doing. And I mean you're going to make a positive celebratory change, not a negative change that punishes you. For example, I often say, "Well, babe, you get to celebrate yourself at the end of the day. What are five things you *did* do right today?"'

Battling self-doubt is a lifelong task for many of us, of course, but Darcel is on a mission to show new mums that it's work that will benefit them and their children. Darcel wants women to treat motherhood as an opportunity to explore, do things differently, live in a more authentic way. Rather than seeing it as a role that inhibits women, she sees it as a portal to self-discovery. A new mum is a person who can choose metamorphosis, like the caterpillar who's 'channelling butterfly energy' even as they turn to goo, only to re-emerge more beautiful than ever. So many women in our community tell us about wanting to parent differently, create a different family dynamic, break the chains of generational trauma and be authentically themselves, for their children's sake as well as their own. Darcel is a cheerleader for these women, and for every woman who dares to be her full self.

She also coaches people to think about growth in terms of integration. Working with the idea that we all contain many aspects and versions, many of them younger and more vulnerable, she invites mums to extend the same loving parenting they offer their kids to these aspects of themselves. Remember Daisy V.-V., who felt there were two versions of herself after she became a mother, the pre-baby and post-baby one? Darcel would invite her to create a dialogue between them, speaking silently or aloud about their wants and needs, inhabiting both in turn. This might sound odd, but it's really about giving a voice to the parts of yourself that don't normally get to be heard.

Darcel explains how it might go: 'In this moment, what is it you truly need? What does your inner child need? How about the version of you who's used to being told, *You're wrong*. Perhaps you know that one of your selves needs a hug, or encouragement. Go ahead. Give her what she needed but didn't receive, whether that's hugging yourself or putting your hand on your heart and just breathing, checking in with your body or offering words of affirmation.'

When we're on a mission to care for our children and support their journey to independence, our own personal journey to wholeness becomes even more crucial. How can you welcome as many aspects of your being as possible?

Becoming a mother divided my life into before and after. I lost some parts of my identity but I gained many more. I made a conscious choice to take full responsibility for my shortcomings and I feel more powerful and more mature now. I'm growing up alongside my child and it feels like a gift.

— **Yana K., US**

You are perfectly good enough already

There are dangers to thinking that we need constant self-improvement. We risk missing out on the here and now if we defer enjoyment and self-value until we've achieved just one more goal. That's not what Darcel is advocating or what mums tell us makes them feel most authentically themselves. Valuing ourselves today, imperfect as we are, is a surer way to authenticity and wholeness.

It's important to recognize that it's easier to value yourself as a good enough mother, partner, friend, leader, sister, performer, *whatever* if you're having at least some positive experiences, are receiving ongoing support and have the resources to do this inner work. Not everybody does. But we hope that hearing from so many women about their doubts and their happiness, their sense of frustration and their fulfilment, has given you inspiration to be curious about how much joy and wholeness there might be for you, as a mother and a person.

In a nutshell . . .

Becoming a mother means dealing with a lot of baggage in the form of assumptions, prejudices and clichés. Some of them will be your own. Your family, your culture, your religion, your community, your friends, the internet and your partner will also have their own understanding of what it means. There are very few labels for a person more loaded than 'mother'. So if it takes you a while (we mean months, possibly years) to figure out how you want to be a mum, that's fair enough. It might be hard, but hopefully it will also be funny, interesting and unexpected – in good ways.

Having mixed feelings about becoming a mother is completely normal, especially when your children are babies and toddlers and you're still adjusting to the huge changes in your sense of identity, values and priorities. Most people find it gradually gets easier to integrate being a mama into their sense of self. If that's not the way it goes for you and you're distressed or frustrated, speak to someone – either a friend or a professional. You won't be the only one who's still wondering who the hell they are now. Talking it over can help you make sense of what you need and want.

Being yourself is an act of self-love that brings joy to the people who love you. You can be a role model for your children by modelling imperfection, self-acceptance and curiosity about what's possible for you. How wild and wonderful can motherhood be in your life? Could it feel like completion, transformation, metamorphosis, integration . . . evolution?

CHAPTER 16

The only way is up, right?

*On the long haul, truly tough
times and raising a villager*

Motherhood is a lifelong job. The first couple of years are intense but hopefully, over time, you figure out how to be the mother you want to be for your particular child. Gradually, families rearrange themselves as they adapt to their new dynamic. But of course kids and life itself are unpredictable. There will always be new challenges. Perhaps you have more children, or your children begin to show signs of developmental issues or health problems. The invisible load of admin and emotional work that comes along with caring for your family never gets lighter, and all the while you're still trying to figure out how to meet your children's needs while also being yourself. There's a moment, different for every mum, when she looks up and realizes that there are another 15, 20 years of this ahead of her. Maybe more. Mums are in it for the long haul.

Samantha Granados is 35 and lives in Kansas City, Missouri, with her husband Selvin and their three children, who are 14, 12 and 5. Her eldest child was diagnosed with ADHD when he was five years old. 'Ryan was a happy baby, very energetic, easy to please, not difficult at all,' says Sam.

'When he was four, I started to notice that he was easily distracted. A year later the kindergarten teacher raised some concerns about his learning. He wasn't making progress with reading, he struggled to follow simple instructions and always treated everything as a joke. Our new paediatrician asked if we'd ever had him tested for ADHD.'

Sure enough, Ryan was diagnosed with impulsive ADHD and then anxiety. The doctors prescribed various different medications including Adderall and Ritalin, but the side effects were awful. He lost weight, he was vacant, and his mood and behaviour grew more troubled. It was only when he was about seven that they settled on guanfacine, which Ryan took for a number of years. He's no longer taking medication. It's relatively common for ADHD symptoms in boys to mellow when they hit puberty, Sam explained. 'When Ryan was 12, he asked if he could stop and we agreed, as long as he does well in school and there's no return of the behaviour issues he had when he was younger.'

Sam says that securing the educational support Ryan needs has been one of the most frustrating and upsetting things. 'The school had to do their own assessments, and that process was very draining. Ryan was nine years old and they were using an assessment system designed for high-school students. They concluded that he was suicidal, though his own psychiatrist did not agree. At one point the school reported me to Missouri social services for neglect. That was the toughest period. We needed to have hard conversations with Ryan about his behaviour, we were at loggerheads with the school and my daughter was about to start there. I didn't want them to assume that she would have the same difficulties as her brother.'

Balancing Ryan's needs with those of her other children

has been a persistent feature of Sam's parenting. 'At home I'm constantly thinking about how to support Ryan while also parenting my two other children and treating all three of them in a balanced way. For example, a lot of children with ADHD hyperfocus on what their peers are doing when they're in trouble, to deflect attention from themselves. Ryan used to do that a lot, especially with his sister, and get very frustrated. He would say we were favouring her or holding him to higher standards. It's got a lot better as he's grown up, but I'm still not sure whether he's really understood that different people have different needs and views. The other hard thing has been strangers making comments about Ryan's behaviour without knowing his circumstances. Even now I sometimes have to tell him "That's not appropriate" when we're at the store, and we'll get looks or comments from other people. I'm much more graceful with myself and with him these days, though. They have no idea what we go through, so we'll take it in our stride.'

Sam's experience of parenting a neurodivergent child shows us that while babies and toddlers can be tough, older kids also come with their own unique challenges. She speaks with assurance about experiences that any of us would find frightening or stressful, from being told our child was at risk of self-harm and having to be an advocate for his needs, to being reported to social services. 'My parenting is not going to be perfect every day,' she says. 'Some days I'm going to be the best mother on earth and then other days, especially with my teenagers, they're not going to understand why I'm their mother when their best friend's mom is so much better. But the longer you do this, the more confident you become – with strangers, family and the kids themselves.'

Sam's the kind of person we'd like to ask for advice on

coping with toddlers, preschoolers and beyond. She's got the longer-term and deeper perspective that reassures us that, even in tough circumstances, the only way is up. Sam smiles when she says, 'Most of the time these days I chalk up Ryan's behaviour to being a teenager. He can get a little mouthy, but it's not like the anger before. My daughter's basically a teen now too. I've learned that a teenager is like a toddler with an opinion. Same moodiness, same drive to be independent. It's just that now they can tell you exactly what they think of you.' Sam's perspective is a reminder that it can be so beneficial to make connections with mums who are a few stages ahead of you, as well as your contemporaries down in the trenches.

Whether you're parenting toddlers or teens or both, being a mama is the definition of a long-term, day-in-day-out undertaking. There will always be some new challenge, but the joys and rewards also continue to accumulate as your children learn to talk, tell you jokes, reveal the contents of their brilliant imaginations and generally grow into the amazing individuals they are. Some of the sleeping, cleaning and feeding work gets easier as they become more independent, but their social struggles might get more complex as they move away from you and out into the world of their peers. As ever, the hard bits are easier to tackle in community and the hilarious and loving bits are even more delightful when you can share them. By the time they're going to nursery, they'll be making friends and you'll have to start running their social lives as well as your own. You might well find that there's ever more overlap between the two. Even if you don't immediately make lifelong buddies, building a support crew to share information, arrange playdates and cover pick-up emergencies can solve logistical headaches and seed a social group for you and your children as you and the village get to know each other.

When every day is daunting

There's a lot to enjoy as our children grow up and we settle into our groove. Generally speaking, the only way is up, even if there will always be hard days. But for mums like Sam, whose children have specific complex needs, the baby years can feel easy compared to what comes later when emotional dysregulation, learning difficulties or behaviour issues can make themselves apparent. If your child has health or developmental issues or your background and circumstances have exposed you to particular disadvantages, the long haul is extra tough. It can place a huge, ongoing strain on your mothering resources.

Susie Stafford's daughter Victoria is now four years old and has just started primary school in Manchester, UK. Victoria has epilepsy and a rare sleep disorder, which means that Susie is her full-time carer. Susie's family live relatively nearby and have supported her practically and emotionally throughout her journey into motherhood, which has been beset by hardship from the beginning. Susie is a single parent and a survivor of sexual violence. She and Victoria recently moved in with her new partner, who's very supportive but isn't well himself. Day-to-day life is focused on meeting Victoria's complex needs.

'Initially she was a strong walker,' Susie explains, 'but then she started having clumsy drop falls. We were living at my parents' house at the time and we all just thought it would sort itself out. Then, at two, Victoria started having shaking episodes. I took her to the hospital emergency department several times, but the shaking would always stop by the time we saw a doctor. I was only 20 years old and I felt the doctors didn't believe me when I told them what was happening. It wasn't until she was two and a half and she had a really violent shaking fit that we managed to get her to hospital in time for a doctor to see it. I wasn't with her. I had gone abroad with a friend for my first holiday since I had her. My daughter was staying with my parents, who took her to hospital. That was absolutely terrifying. I rushed back in a total panic.

'In some ways it's helped to have the diagnosis, but her condition isn't under control yet. The doctors are still looking for the right drug regime. I'm frightened for her safety all the time. She has a lot of very short daily seizures, like momentary blackouts. They can happen anywhere – as we're crossing a road, when she's on top of a climbing frame, on the bus – and they cause her to lose control of her body and fall. She's not aware of them happening at the time and has only recently begun to understand that she has a serious illness. I can't work because I need to be available if anything happens at school, and to care for her the rest of the time.'

Susie worries a lot but says it's nothing like the despair she experienced before she had her daughter. 'She won't be able to go on playdates or for sleepovers unless the medication starts to work. And in any case, I'm very anxious about safeguarding. There aren't many support groups for parents of children with epilepsy, and due to my anxiety, I would struggle to go to them anyway. I have my parents and partner to support me, but life is very tiring and stressful. My daughter keeps me going. Being pregnant with her probably saved me from doing something bad. Now I believe it's all made me stronger, so I can be here for her.'

Susie is articulate, self-composed and extraordinarily open-hearted, considering the discrimination and indifference she's had to cope with from police, the legal system and the medical establishment as she battles for her daughter's wellbeing and struggles to heal from her own trauma. When we talked to her, she was going over Victoria's care plan for her first day at primary school. Susie's spirit and determination to keep on keeping on were obvious. She's in it for the long haul and focused on making sure that the only way really is up.

Most of us won't have to face the level of challenge that Susie and her daughter are up against, but all of us will have crises and hard times as our babies turn into toddlers who turn into preschoolers. We'll all be sending our child off to school one day soon. Our role as their mother will continue to be crucial. We'll be on call for accidents, fallings-out with friends, learning difficulties, bullying – whatever the future brings. We're raising our child and raising ourselves as we go. It's never too late in our motherhood journey to find and build our village of supporters, cheerleaders, advisers, babysitters and allies so we can share the wild ride.

Culture gaps and family baggage

As they grow up, our children become villagers alongside us and start to have relationships with many more people. They need our help to learn how to relate to family members and the wider community, and how to communicate and behave appropriately in different contexts. Language and culture become new potential flashpoints for conflict, as well as learning opportunities.

Sam's children are growing up exposed to two languages: Spanish as well as English – though she's very funny about her husband's hit-and-miss approach to actually speaking Spanish with their kids. Multilingual families are increasingly common all over the world, which can bring incredible advantages but also make parenting and family life that little bit more challenging. Aside from the sometimes fraught struggle to run a bilingual household, there's extra potential for tension with extended families if there are different cultural backgrounds, and managing these tensions often falls on the woman – yet more invisible labour.

Many women in our community live abroad or have a partner who's a different nationality to them, or both. This can have a huge impact in terms of loneliness and lack of support but also on our ability to settle into our new role and family dynamic. We may be navigating unfamiliar customs, a different language, or friends and family who have different expectations. All of that can make it harder to find our village.

Kerry says she's still not sure where she fits in, even after three years living in the US and despite the common language. 'I can't really speak as a British mum even though I'm British and a mum, because I've not had a child in the UK. Then again, I don't feel like an American mum either. My husband is Asian-American. His mum is Taiwanese, his dad is Chinese. Our son is learning Mandarin as well as English, and I'm also trying to learn. We celebrate British, American and Asian holidays. It's actually great fun, but it does add another layer of complexity to my already confused identity!'

I'm English and have moved to the Netherlands to be with my partner. I definitely suffered with postnatal depression, alongside grieving my country. Becoming a mum has brought so much to my life, but I'm in a very confusing time of finding myself in this new place and new phase.

— Sasha S., Netherlands

Danielle Manzella is also Asian-American, married to an Italian-American husband. 'Italian and Asian cultures are both very family-oriented, which has been helpful, but there are still differences between me and my husband. I'm much more into tradition and cultural knowledge than he is. I want my son to know where he's come from, on both sides. I grew up in a huge extended family, with all of us going to my Chinese grandmother's house every weekend. The whole family was raising the children and there were expectations for each child. My younger aunt, for example, raised her own kids in my grandma's house. But my husband didn't grow up in a traditional extended Italian family, and I feel like he doesn't understand the importance of it. He says, "Why are you guys doing it so big? Why can't we have it just be us?" His parents totally understand, though. They've actually gone to my mom's for holidays like Thanksgiving and vice versa. They like the sense of belonging.'

Danielle, her husband and their five-year-old son have lived in her Italian in-laws' house in a small town in Massachusetts since just before their child was born. 'My husband and I have been together since we graduated high school. We were never sure whether we wanted children until there was a "now or never" moment in my mid-thirties. I got pregnant easily but then had a miscarriage, and it was another year before I got pregnant again. When the pandemic landed, we moved in with my in-laws. We hadn't planned it that way, but it felt like what I was used to. And then I had my son at 32 weeks. He was in the NICU for a month before coming home, and once we had a preemie baby, well, we really leaned heavily on his grandparents for practical help and emotional support. Living with them was a godsend. And we've just kind of stayed. They have similar values to us and they're careful about not stepping on toes. My son's an only child so it's important to me that he has a lot of contact with his grandparents, aunts, uncles and cousins on both sides. It works really well for us.'

Danielle's family is a great advert for multigenerational living, cross-cultural family understanding and the benefits of having your village close, especially in tough times. We won't all have or want that particular set-up, but there are always ways to engineer a little more of the elements that we do value. It might be contact with peers for an only child or staying in touch with cultural roots; being exposed to your family's language or tradition or showing your child that people from different backgrounds can thrive together. Whatever your values, raising your child as a villager is full of opportunities for you, for them and for your community.

Coming out the other side

The long haul of motherhood is a complicated journey with multiple stages. Danielle is honest about it having taken five years to figure out who she is now, even though she's had a ton of practical and emotional support from her folks, her in-laws and her partner. 'It sounds kind of crazy, but I feel like I'm just starting to rediscover and redefine myself. I finally know who I am as a person. I've come out the other end of those early years when it's all-consuming. One of my old friends, who isn't a mother herself, has been instrumental in me feeling like I'm coming to the end of one period of mothering and entering another. She's stuck by me, carried on inviting me to adult social events as well as coming to kid-focused stuff with me and my son. She's content with being the really cool auntie. She gets all of the fun stuff and then goes back to being a career woman and doing her thing. She's given me a sense of continuity with my old life and I think I've given her an opportunity to play a role that she loves.'

We love that Danielle and her old friend have forged an alliance that's nurtured both of them in different ways and given her son another perspective on the world and women's role within it. We absolutely love to see women supporting women through tough times and everyday challenges, across generations and cultures. There's a role for everyone. When we parent in the village, among family and friends, everyone benefits.

In a nutshell . . .

Motherhood is a marathon, not a sprint. For many of us it does get gradually easier overall as we settle into our role and grow in confidence, but there will always be new challenges. For some of us, especially if our children have extra needs or our situation is highly pressured, those challenges can be very significant. Whatever you're dealing with, if you're still struggling or are struggling more than ever, keep looking for the support you need. Seek out mums who are a little bit further along in the marathon. It's never too late to find your village.

Part of the job is teaching your child how to be a villager. This can be a joy, an opportunity and a challenge as you navigate questions about behaviour, language and culture. You might find yourself dealing with a lot of invisible labour as you distil different values and expectations from family and friends. Try to share the burden where you can and cut yourself some slack if this turns out to be an intense learning period for you as well as your child.

Keep prioritizing you. No matter how long you've been a mum, you will still have bad days and the societal, emotional, physical and economic pressures on you as a mother haven't gone away. So remember to prioritize your own needs and resist the mum guilt.

CHAPTER 17

I think I'm actually getting the hang of this!

On learning to thrive in the village

At some point, and it looks different and arrives at a different time for everyone, you will realize that the balance has shifted. You're finally a little more peaceful than you are stressed, more confident than you are anxious. You're not 'a perfect mum' and you know she doesn't exist. You're *the* perfect mum for your little one, and for your life. It's a beautiful moment when you can embrace motherhood and your new family life and love it for all its imperfections. Finally, you're actually getting the hang of all this.

> My daughter was born after four rounds of IVF and still feels like a miracle. She's teaching me so much wisdom and strength just by being herself. Every evening we name three things we're grateful for that day, so now I look out for glimmers of inspiration so I can share them with her. She makes me so proud and so determined to nurture myself. I take sea dips every week, I meditate, do yoga and journalling. She's made me see that I'm worth more than I had ever believed.
>
> — **Caroline E., UK**

We believe that every mother deserves to thrive in motherhood. There are as many ways to do that as there are mums — as the beautiful chorus of voices in this book shows. But however you define your particular version of thriving, flourishing and loving your life, we sincerely wish that you feel fully yourself, reach your potential and fulfil your roles, all while enjoying the journey. It won't feel that glorious every day, but of course you know that. Mamas are expert at rolling with the punches, finding the positive while staying realistic.

> *Motherhood has opened my eyes to the beauty of the world. I've worked through a lot of mental health issues and I'm proud of myself. Plus, I've already made so many wonderful friends on this journey. I'm determined to break generational curses for my daughter's sake, and I'm feeling confident that with the support I'm fortunate to have, I can do it.*
>
> **— Jade H., UK**

Motherhood makes women brave and pushes them to make big changes. Two years after her child was born, Daisy V.-V. from the US became a substitute teacher and is now working her way towards a full-time career in education. 'I figured I'd be able to bring to it all the patience I've learned since becoming a parent.'

Motherhood also makes women open-hearted and generous, especially towards other mothers. We are inspired every day by the community spirit and solidarity we see springing up all over the world. Destinie Guzman is building community among mums in New York City. Like many people, she's partly motivated by wanting to give to others what she couldn't find when she had her child. 'When I was starting out making friends, the group chats I was in got messy. It felt like some people were bullying others. That's not the energy I want. I want people to feel good. I know how it feels to be down and I don't want that for these women. They're great moms, they're my girls and they deserve the world.'

There are 30 people in the group that Destinie has brought together. They meet up, pool resources so they can go on picnics with the kids, babysit for one another, go out for drinks. It's been the support that Destinie needed as she figures out housing and employment, separates from her child's dad and finishes school. Creating her own village of mums has allowed Destinie and her daughter to flourish, despite the challenges. 'I feel like I'm starting to find my place. I didn't have that for so long. I had a lot going on, dealing with mental health problems and school and everything. And now all those things are floating away. I'm learning what works for me and my daughter. She's my top priority but I'm realizing that I'm a priority too.'

Becoming a mother made me feel complete. I realized I can impact the world in profound ways by raising smart, amazing kids. Some days I feel like a personal assistant to three demanding bosses, but life is full of joy and wonder. I'm blessed to have support from my now husband, and amazing friends who bring a village to help me with the kids and with my needs.

— Elizabeth K., US

Women supporting women in a non-judgemental community has been Peanut's whole mission right from day one; we know that it truly can deliver life-changing benefits. When mums are parenting in a village of people they trust, it's much easier for them and their children to thrive, despite any external barriers to their wellbeing. Mums are resilient, powerful and resourceful. When we raise each other up, there's nothing we can't do.

One of the most inspiring stories we've ever heard in our community shows exactly how mums can transform heartbreak into connection and build their village by reaching out to one another with compassion. Vanessa S. is a mother of three, with two children who are now three and four, and one who was stillborn. She lives in Charlotte, North Carolina, and is British, married to her American husband. She had been in the US for less than a year when she fell pregnant with her first child. 'It was lonely being pregnant without my village,' she says. 'I was a long way from London, where I grew up. I was happy to be in the US, but we didn't know anyone in Charlotte when we arrived, so I was starting from scratch.'

When Vanessa's first son was stillborn at 40 weeks, her grief and trauma were magnified by the lack of a support network. 'My mum came over for the birth and was going to stay to help us for a few weeks. She thought she'd be welcoming her first grandson. Instead, she was supporting me to cope with the most devastating pain I've ever experienced. When Mum went back to London, I was pretty much on my own aside from my partner, who obviously was also grieving. My sister came over for a week and then my older brother visited, but in terms of having people around on a day-to-day basis, we just didn't have anyone.'

Vanessa was in shock. 'I said to the doctor, *How can this happen?* I didn't even know that you could get all the way to full term without problems and then lose your baby. She told me that it's more common than you realize; people just don't talk about it.'

Vanessa and her husband supported each other, communicating honestly and openly, bringing kindness to all their interactions; somehow, they pulled through. Vanessa became pregnant again, and her rainbow baby was born 12 months later, to be joined by his sister a year and a half after that. 'I knew that I needed mum friends,' Vanessa says, 'but I was also nervous because I'd had this very specific experience and, even though people are kind, it's hard for them to really understand what I went through. So just after my living son was born, I turned to Peanut, and I was able to find other mums who had experienced child loss and stillbirth. I connected with a lady who lives in Charlotte who had been through the same thing, and I joined groups where I could share my feelings and support other women going through something similar. It changed everything for me.'

Vanessa is a keen baker and had been making and selling cakes on and off for ten years by the time she lost her son. In the aftermath, when the shock and agony were at their most raw, she picked it up again. 'It was therapeutic. I didn't have to speak to anyone and it helped me to feel a little more grounded. And I really enjoy giving people cupcakes. The look on someone's face when they receive freshly baked cupcakes is so wonderful to see. I put the two things together and came up with an idea.'

Every Mother's Day since she lost her first son, Vanessa's suffering has been extra intense. After her second son was born, she asked herself how she could prepare for the next one. Her inspiration was to do something to help other women in her community who were also struggling with grief and trauma on Mother's Day, whether from child loss or other causes. 'I decided to bake cupcakes and deliver them to mums who need them. But I wasn't sure how to go about it. So I reached out to Peanut and said, I've got this idea but

I'm not sure how to start. They helped me to build the frame-work for Cupcakes for Compassion, and I've done it for three years now. Any mum in Charlotte can nominate another mum who's in need of a little compassion on Mother's Day. I bake the cakes, decorate them, box them up, write out the note from the nominator and then deliver the cupcakes to the mum on their doorstep. My husband helps me fold boxes and does some deliveries. It really stirs up my emotions, but it's helped me so much and I know it helps other mums because they write and tell me so. Once upon a time, I was that person who just wished that someone could relate to my experience. I've discovered a whole community of mums who know how tough Mother's Day can be, and I love that we've been able to support each other.'

We couldn't be more inspired by Vanessa's story. We've always believed that a moment of connection between mums can be the foundation on which a community is built. To see Vanessa building her village one cupcake delivery at a time is the most beautiful reminder that there is nothing as powerful for healing, supporting and nurturing women and their children as a network of mums who've got each other's back.

We hope you've been inspired by the stories you've heard. If you're struggling, we hope you've felt seen and found some relief in knowing that you're not alone. If you opened the book looking for honesty about the highs as well as the lows of motherhood, we hope you found it. And if you're wonder-ing how to build the village you need, we hope you've picked up ideas from the women who've been there and done that.

Peanut Pro Darcel Being, who has created a thriving online group of mums supporting each other to live wholeheartedly, is a firm believer that we can all find our village. Some of us find it through prenatal classes, others through chatting to mums we meet in the playground. Some of us rely on our family, others on our old friends. We might find it in our church or a specific parents' support group. Many of us will find support across a number of different groups as our needs change. At every point, the key thing is to go looking for our people and then be prepared to give our time and energy to the group.

'A village only flourishes if everybody contributes,' Darcel says. 'It can be no other way. And there's such a mutual benefit, because the more you give, the more capacity you have to receive. In the giving, you find that you have more space and feel better in making an ask.' As Destinie's experience shows, when we give others the help we would wish to receive ourselves, we create the space and the community we all need.

Darcel helps women to identify what they can offer to the communities they're already in, or to kick-start a community they want to grow. 'What is it you are most passionate about? What annoys you the most? What are you judging the most? That will point you to the need that you're being called to serve in. Get really clear on *how* you want to serve. What do you want to offer to the group? If you know that mums are stressed, could you host a regular breathwork session? If it's companionship, could you host a coffee morning in a cafe? Whatever it is, be clear and be realistic about what you can contribute. And then, be brave – try it. Reach out and offer something to someone. The village has everything to gain, and so do you.'

Dr Lisa Folden also encourages women to create connections with one another and favours mutual celebration of even tiny successes. She suggests that offering a fellow mum a compliment can be the start of a journey towards creating the village that will benefit both of you. 'I find that women don't know how to celebrate themselves. If someone says something nice about us, we tend to bat it away. That goes double for mums. But to compliment someone sincerely is to offer them a gift. When we accept it, we form a connection with that person. That creates the possibility of so much more understanding, encouragement, motivation, comfort. And when we tell our stories and talk about our experiences honestly and with kindness, we give everyone else permission to do the same and to learn from one another.'

That's the village, right there. It flourishes through random kindness and unexpected connections and is built with generosity of spirit. We hope you find the village you need to support you to thrive, flourish, love and laugh along your motherhood journey. You absolutely deserve it.

Love,
Team Peanut

Acknowledgements

This book exists thanks to the millions of women who are part of the Peanut community, women who have courageously shared their stories, both joyful and challenging, in the hope of making someone else's journey just a little bit easier. So that the mums out there feeling isolated or uncertain can be reminded that they are never alone, and that everything will be all right.

Heartfelt thanks to Helen and Phoebe, who brought together the voices of remarkable women and mothers from around the world, weaving their stories into something truly special.

And to the entire Peanut team: thank you for creating and nurturing this extraordinary community. Your passion and dedication make it possible for these connections to thrive and inspire every day.

Finally, Finlay and Nuala. You are my world. You teach me how to be a mummy every day, and everything is for you. I love you.

And RT, for making me brave even when I feel tiny. Ani l'dodi.

With love and admiration always,

Michelle x

Index